# AROUND THE WORLD IN A DUTCH OVEN

HOBBLE CREEK PRESS
AN IMPRINT OF CEDAR FORT, INC.
SPRINGVILLE, UTAH

ISBN 13: 978-1-59955-972-8

Published by Hobble Creek Press, an imprint of Cedar Fort, Inc.
2373 W. 700 S., Springville, UT 84663
Distributed by Cedar Fort, Inc., www.cedarfort.com

Library of Congress Cataloging-in-Publication Data on file

Cover design and cover photography by Erica Dixon
Cover design © 2013 by Lyle Mortimer
Edited by Aubrey Luddington and Casey J. Winters

Printed in the United States of America

10 9 8 7 6 5 4 3 2 1

**TO JODI, BRENDON, AND JACOB**

# CONTENTS

## What This Book Showcases

**THROUGHOUT MY LIFE,** people have used many different words to describe me. Some of them, I'm happy to say, are quite nice. Others, not so much. Among those that are not often used to describe me are

- Typical
- Normal
- Average
- Usual
- Expected
- Mainstream

This is, I think, mostly due to a rebellious streak in me, instilled by my mother. She will probably deny any responsibility, but, truly, she is either the source of it or, at the very least, the inspiration. All of my life I have tried to be different, separate from what was common.

As I first started to explore Dutch oven cooking, I tried a lot of the traditional dishes, but I also wanted to stretch beyond that. I wanted to try things that didn't commonly turn up at a Dutch oven cook-off or gathering.

I tried recipes from fancier cookbooks and dishes from other continents and cuisines. I soon discovered, as I cooked more and more, that there were many other Dutch oven chefs like me—those who liked to surprise, who liked to dazzle their guests. I soon discovered that virtually *anything* can be cooked in a Dutch oven. A dish might need some adaptation, and some dishes need to be adapted more than others, but they all can be done!

Over the years on my blog at marksblackpot.com, I've tried to find and attempt many things that I felt were out of the mainstream of "typical" or "traditional" Dutch oven cooking. This book is a compilation of many of those recipes. Here, you'll find dishes that are a little more complex, a little fancier, a little more exotic, and made with more challenging techniques. You'll find a lot of dishes from all over the world (I've hit every continent, except for Antarctica, of course).

I hope I've explained in this book how I did the cooking in such a way as to make the recipes easy to do. That way, even a less-experienced but still adventurous chef could pull them off! If you're not feeling confident, you might want to try my other book *Black Pot for Beginners* first, available at marksblackpot.com or cedarfort.com. If you follow the steps of study and practice found there, you'll certainly be able to tackle any of the dishes in this book!

Also, as I've been learning to be a better and better chef over the years, I've been exploring cooking as expression, cooking as a way to look inside yourself and surprise yourself. Cooking can be a form of art, and in the bonus chapters at the end I've included some of the challenges and exercises that I've tried to help me be more artistic in my own cooking.

So . . . come travel with me, come explore with me, come learn with me!

## World Peace

I've often thought that if you truly wanted world peace, you'd get everyone together for one huge pot luck. We'd all bring our traditional dishes, our most humble and most fancy feasts, and we'd all sit down and try each other's food. And we'd have a great time at this huge, worldwide dinner party. By knowing each other's foods, we'd know a bit more about each other and find mutual respect and even friendship. What a wonderful and tasty world that would be!

But then I think that someone would probably bring sautéed scorpion on a stick, and I'm not sure how I would handle that.

But the sentiment of the idea is still cool, don't cha think? And since it would be logistically impossible to set up a dinner table big enough for the whole world, I'll do the next best thing for me and my family and bring as much of their dinner table to mine as I can.

Contemporary American culture is young (as cultures go), so we've had to build it up from fragments and ideas of all of the cultures that have fed into it. Since early in our nation's history, there have been influences from Europe, Africa, Asia, and the natives who were here all along.

The end result, which fascinates me so much, is that we in the United States now have a rich culinary heritage that has grown and fused from all of these lands.

I love tasting and testing world foods. I love learning that little bit of the culture. I love seeing how available ingredients develop into regional combinations and ultimately into a cuisine.

I also enjoy seeing how dishes and cooking styles meld, blend, and fuse as people travel the world more and more. Fine dining and folk restaurants adapt traditional dishes both to the ingredients available in the new host location and to the palates of the populace around them.

Which leads me to talk a little bit about another topic . . .

## Thoughts on "Authenticity"

The Dutch oven, in spite of being named "Dutch," is inseparably tied to the history of the United States. From the days of early colonial life on the East Coast, to the days of the wild frontier in the Midwest, to the westward migrations and the famous cattle drives of the Old West, the Dutch oven was there to see it all and feed people along the way.

So who do I think I am, doing a Brazilian barbacoa, an Asian stir-fry, a European pasta, or a curry from India? How can I possibly think to make it "authentic"?

Okay, you got me. I can't.

I'm not from any of those cultures, and I don't know the depths of generations of handed-down cooking techniques. I don't have any special tools and ovens specific to that cuisine. I have an American cast-iron black pot, not a tandoor!

But that's not going to keep me from trying to get it as close as I can! That won't stop me from tasting new flavors and learning a new technique or skill. I'd encourage you to explore the world through eating and cooking!

There are purists who will say that if it's not being made by an old Sicilian lady, then it's not real Italian food, or if the ingredients weren't bought from a small corner Asian market, it's not real Thai. I confess I've got mixed feelings. On the one hand, I do applaud any effort to be as true to the original as possible; on the other hand, I also recognize practicalities. Do it as close as you can, and let taste be the ultimate judge.

# What Is "Gourmet"?

I'm having trouble using the word "gourmet" to describe either the recipes in this book or myself as a chef. This is mostly because I don't really know what it means for something or someone to be "gourmet."

Here's what Dictionary.com has to say about it:

> **gour·met** [goor-mey]
> *noun*
> **1.** a connoisseur of fine food and drink; epicure.
>
> *adjective*
> **2.** of or characteristic of a gourmet, especially in involving or purporting to involve high-quality or exotic ingredients and skilled preparation: *gourmet meals*; *gourmet cooking.*
>
> **3.** elaborately equipped for the preparation of fancy, specialized, or exotic meals: *a gourmet kitchen.*

Great. So who decides what "purports" to be "high-quality"? What is a "connoisseur"? An "epicure"?

> **con·nois·seur** [kon-uh-sur, -soor]
> *noun*
> **1.** a person who is especially competent to pass critical judgments in an art, particularly one of the fine arts, or in matters of taste: *a connoisseur of modern art.*
>
> **2.** a discerning judge of the best in any field: *a connoisseur of horses.*
>
> **ep·i·cure** [ep-i-kyoor]
> *noun*
> **1.** a person who cultivates a refined taste, especially in food and wine; connoisseur.

See? We're just running in circles here. What it basically comes down to is this: Anyone that wants to label anyone or anything as "gourmet" is pretty much free to do so. And, as a result, that word has pretty much lost its meaning.

I certainly don't pretend to be a "gourmet" chef, although some of the things I've cooked have tasted as good as or even better than things I've spent a lot of money for in nice restaurants. I don't pretend to know a "gourmet" dish from a "lowbrow" or "peasant" dish, but I know that in my life and travels, I've tasted some delicious things from both humble and elaborate kitchens.

I do strive for the best in my cooking, and I do constantly try to learn more techniques and expose myself to more and more flavors and cuisines. My blog and my books have always been my way of sharing that. If I can help someone else along the way, that's great!

## Is Cooking "Art"?

On my blog, I've talked before about what makes a work "art." I've said that my definition of "art" is that when experiencing true art, it makes me think or feel something new, or in a new way. That can mean a lot of things. Maybe I just admire the brushstrokes on a painting, and it makes me think of how dedicated the artist was. Maybe I get a new interpretation on an older, more familiar work. Maybe I get a spiritual insight that hadn't occurred to me before.

But that's always been from the point of view of the viewer, the consumer of the work. What about from the perspective of the artist? What defines "art" then? And does cooking fit that definition?

Well, art, from the artist's point of view, would have to come from something new. To simply follow a recipe, a formula, or a premade pattern wouldn't be art.

It would have to come from somewhere inside me, to help me discover something new about myself. It would have to allow me to express.

And, finally, it would have to connect with an audience, a consumer, in some way. And I think it would be more "artistic" if it connected on a deeper level than "Oh, that's nice," or even "That sure tastes good!"

So, yes, I think that cooking can qualify as art on those three levels. It certainly doesn't always. I do like to modify recipes and to even create new ones. I don't know that anything that I've ever cooked in my Dutch oven has ever caused a new thought or an inspiration. But it is something I can aspire to.

Anyway, if it *is* an art form, it strikes me as interesting. It would be one of the few art forms where enjoying the art in it's fullest way involves destroying it.

Also, it would be one of the few art forms that would have evolved from

something that is fundamentally essential for survival—eating. Granted, food doesn't have to be artistically prepared to provide nourishment, but then, you don't need to go to the theater or have paintings on your wall to survive either.

Food as art also has to be more than just the visual arrangement of things on the plate. The taste and the smells, the combinations of ingredients, and the techniques used must produce a result that resonates with both the chef and the taster. It's definitely something to aspire to and to strive for, but I don't think it happens often, even for the most experienced of chefs. And that would make it something to be celebrated whenever it does!

## Learning About Flavors
### (or, NOT EVERYTHING TASTES LIKE CHICKEN)

I hope you don't mind, but I'm going to get a little "heady" for a bit. I hope it's ultimately helpful to you as well.

One night recently, I was out at a restaurant with my wife, and she smiled one of her knowing smiles and pointed out the irony in the dish I had ordered. It had both broccoli and asparagus—vegetables I had hated as a kid. Not just disliked, either, but violently rejected. And now, here, I had ordered a plate with both of them combined, and I was happily eating them.

I've been doing a lot of thought and study about flavors lately. For a long time, I've wondered what makes me like some things and not others. And why the things I can't stand are things that others love. Why did I hate some things as a kid and like them now?

My study started as I was writing the spices and flavorings chapter of *Black Pot for Beginners*. In it, I suggested mixing individual spices with butter and spreading it on a neutral-tasting bread, to be able to learn what each spice really tastes like. The results often surprised my palate and opened my eyes.

I started thinking about the flavors I was tasting, and I started formulating, in my own mind, a way to analyze and discuss flavors a bit better, mostly as a way to clarify them in my head and to understand a dish better.

That led me to two analogies:

One: As I studied music, lo, these many years ago, I learned that notes are combined to form chords, and that each chord functions in different ways to move the overall song forward. There are names for the functions of the chords: tonic, dominant, subdominant, and so on. This allows musicians to

use a common language when talking about the music. Being able to label things and talk about them helps everyone to understand them better.

Two: In the world of perfumes, the scents that combine to form a perfume are also referred to as "notes." They come out to the senses gradually. Top notes, for example, are the first things you smell when you put on the perfume. It's also what you smell in the store. They can dissipate very quickly. Middle notes come out soon after and transition into the base notes. These come on after about a half hour and linger for the rest of the evening, giving the lasting impression of the perfume. This is the language that master perfumers speak when they're discussing their work.

It occurred to me that these analogies can be applied to the culinary arts as well. The flavors blend like chords and have function in the dish. They can also, in some dishes, come on in layers and even create lasting impressions, even after the dish is eaten.

As I started to think about this, I started thinking about the food I was eating. I started to notice flavors and notice the way those flavors combined. I started eating differently. Or, I should say, I started enjoying it differently as I ate. I started to formulate the words and thoughts to describe the things I was tasting. Those formulations started to coalesce into a more coherent system. I want to show you the system I'm discovering to help me to describe the recipes I'll be writing about.

What I'm talking about is a way to study, analyze, and—ultimately—discuss the flavors I am tasting in a dish. I did a bit of research and reading of other sources and ideas as well. A great book that I strongly recommend to anyone that wants to truly explore cooking is *Culinary Artistry* by Andrew Dornenburg and Karen Page. This book describes a lot about creativity in the world of food, on lots of levels. Great book!

Scientists say that the human tongue can taste four things: sweet, bitter, sour, and salty. There is some debate over a fifth flavor, vaguely named "umami." It's supposed to be a sort of savory flavor.

Those made sense but still felt a little inadequate to describe all the things I thought I could taste. As I was reading, researching, and tasting, I thought I would add a few, some that others suggested in my searching and others that I added on my own. These are not scientific so much as practical. These are things that I sense are elements of dishes I eat. I'm not sure why, but drawing on the analogies I made previously, I think I'd like to call these "tones."

Here they are, with some descriptions:

## MARK'S FLAVOR TONES

### SWEET

This is the obvious first thing to me, since I tend to eat a lot of sweets. I probably shouldn't, or at least, I should make the sweets I eat more healthy, but that's a discussion for another day. This one is at the top of my list because it's one everyone will recognize. Here are some examples of ingredients with sweet tones:

- sugar
- honey
- fruits
- chocolate
- spices that go with sweet: like cinnamon, nutmeg, cloves, ginger (these might not be sweet themselves, but they tend to bring out the sweet tones in a dish, so I include them)

### SAVORY/SALTY

When I started learning to cook, the term "savory" often confused me. I learned to describe it as "Things that were not bitter, sour, or sweet." In most cases, this flavor comes from meats, although many meats also bring some sweet or other tones to the song as well. As I've been formulating this system, I'm learning that all the tones work together and are rarely found in isolation. Here are some examples of savory tones:

- meats
- salts
- spices that go with meats: like paprika, pepper, garlic

### TANGY/SOUR

Things that are tangy or sour usually contain acids. These tones can really liven up a dish! Here are some examples of tangy or sour tones:

- tomatoes
- citrus, especially lemons, though oranges also have sweet tones, and grapefruit have bitter tones as well
- vinegar

## BITTER

The funny thing about bitter tones is that we don't like them. In theory, we developed the ability to taste bitter as a defense mechanism to steer us away from eating poisons and other harmful things. So why would we intentionally cook with these tones? When you combine them with other tones, they add depth, and the whole becomes delicious! There's an analogy to life in there somewhere (speaking of art). Here are some examples of bitter tones:

- some herbs, like parsley
- some spices, like nutmeg or cardamom
- medicines

## SPICY

There are some foods that, evolutionarily speaking, surprise me. Take, for example, an habanero chili pepper. At some point, some prehistoric ancestor of ours took a bite of it. Heat like that would have lit his tongue on fire. It would have felt like it was biting back! So, what thought went through that neanderthal brain that made him want to take a second bite? Or a third? At what point in the epochs did we decide that this feeling was a good thing? I don't know, but I'm glad we did! Here are some examples of spicy tones:

- black pepper
- chili peppers
- cinnamon
- ginger

## COOL

There are very few foods that create the sensation of cool in your mouth, but it is such a distinct sensation that I think it deserves to be labeled as its own tone. Plus, I love it! Here are some examples of cold tones:

- mint
- menthol
- wintergreen

**UNDERTONE**

This is one that I added to the list on my own, not at the suggestion of a book or science. The undertone is like the canvas the painting is painted on, or the quiet background noise that the music plays over. It's the bread of a wonderful sandwich or the pasta to carry a delicious sauce. It's not a strong flavor, and it can be difficult to identify, but you would miss it if it wasn't there. Here are some examples of undertone:

- bread
- rice
- potatoes
- cooked beans

**AS I'VE** started to think of the dishes I taste in terms of these flavor tones, I've found that even mundane eating sometimes becomes an exploration. When I'm paying attention, I start to notice things that were always there but not identified, not in my awareness. Food tastes more interesting!

The Dr Pepper that I'm sipping as I write this, for example, has a strong sour tone, with just enough sweet to make it palatable. There's a hint of bitter there as well, and it fades off into a lingering salty/sour tone.

I don't know if me blathering on about this is helping, but it has been fascinating to me, and thanks for letting me share it. As we travel the world in the next chapters, I hope you find it interesting to see how similar yet distinct the uses for these flavors are, from one continent to the next.

Now, on to the recipes!

# UNITED STATES

**I LOVE** that the United States of America is often referred to as a "Melting Pot." I know that's actually a metallurgical metaphor for culture, but I like to think of it as a culinary observation as well. We're such a large country, geographically, that there are many regions. We're also a diverse country, socially and culturally, that draws from the traditions of the people of many nations that have been drawn here to the "land of opportunity."

Yet, somehow, it's all American food! That's what I love about my country.

## American

### STEAK AND CRAB FEAST

I wanted to do something amazingly, phenomenally over-the-top special for my wedding anniversary one year. At the time, it marked twenty-four years that, day in and day out, my wife hadn't kicked my sorry butt out on the curb. That's cause for celebration. That deserved the best meal I could create.

My wife loves T-bone steaks, so I shopped around, looking for some good, thick porterhouses. I did find some, but they weren't really as thick as I would've liked.

I'd seen some videos on how to pan-fry steak, and I was really interested in that. I started to form an idea in my mind about doing the pan-fry steaks with a spice rub. I figured I would steam some corn on the cob too. Then, I figured I could do some of those garlic-sliced, sesame seed baked potatoes. To top it all off, we had some crab legs in the freezer, so that would make it great too!

Crab would also take us both back to our honeymoon, where we dined, starry-eyed, on crab in a butter sauce.

The challenge for me was to cook it all in a limited time frame. I would be coming home from work by about five, and I would want to have it done when it was still light out. That only gave me a 2–3 hour window to cook and serve the whole meal.

In my planning, I figured out how I would make the ovens work. I would do the corn and the crab together in the 12-inch deep Dutch oven, and the potatoes and the steaks each in their own 12-inch shallow Dutch oven. When planning the time, I started from the end and went through the steps of each dish in my mind, to see when I'd have to start each one.

## THE PAN-FRIED T-BONE STEAKS

### TOOLS
12-inch Dutch oven
26–30 coals below (pack 'em in!)

### INGREDIENTS
*The spice rub:*
1 Tbsp. cumin
1 Tbsp. crushed coriander
1 Tbsp. garlic powder
1 Tbsp. coarse ground black pepper
1 Tbsp. thyme
2 Tbsp. paprika
2 Tbsp. salt
1 tsp. oregano

2–3 T-bone steaks
a little olive oil

1 cup cranberry/grape juice (100 percent juice), at room temperature
1–2 Tbsp. flour dissolved
½ cup water

## THE POTATOES

### TOOLS
12-inch Dutch oven

8–10 coals below
16–18 coals above

**INGREDIENTS**
4–5 medium-to-large potatoes
4–5 cloves garlic
olive oil
kosher salt
sesame seeds

## THE STEAMED CRAB AND CORN ON THE COB

**TOOLS**
12-inch deep Dutch oven
about 20 coals below

**INGREDIENTS**
3–4 cobs of corn
2–3 racks of crab legs
3–4 cups water
½ cup lemon juice

## THE BUTTER DIP/SPREAD FOR THE CRAB/CORN

**TOOLS**
8-inch Dutch oven
10–12 coals below

**INGREDIENTS**
2 cubes butter
extra spice rub (see previous page)

**I STARTED** out with the thawed steaks. Actually, I never froze them in the first place. I brought them home a day or so before and put them straight into the fridge. I mixed up the spices in a zip-top baggie and then added each steak, one at a time. I shook the spices all over the steak and then shook off the excess when I pulled it out. I did the same with the other two steaks. (By the way, this is the same spice mix that I used for my blackened salmon many years ago.)

I set the steaks aside in the fridge, covered in plastic. It would be about another hour before they'd be cooked. That gave the spices plenty of time to set into the meat.

Then I started on the potatoes. The first step was to peel the garlic and slice it into thin slivers. Then I took the potatoes and washed and rinsed them. I cut them almost all the way through in narrow strips so it could fan open a little bit. Then, in every other slice or so, I inserted a sliver of garlic; I alternated between the middle and the right and left sides so it would separate in different and unique ways. (It's tough to describe this process.) As each potato was sliced and garlicked, I put it in the Dutch oven.

Once all the potatoes were prepped, I drizzled each one with a bit of olive oil and then sprinkled kosher salt and sesame seeds over them. It really makes for an impressive display. I put that on the coals to bake.

Next to go was the corn and the crab. I shucked, cleaned, and broke the cobs in half and put them on one of those butterflying steamers in the 12-inch deep Dutch oven. I added the crab on top. I poured in enough water to reach the bottom of the steamer and poured in the lemon juice. I put the lid on and put it on the coals.

The last step was the steaks. I began by putting the 12-inch Dutch oven, with just a little oil, on a lot of coals. I wanted this thing to be seriously hot. Have lots of coals on the side handy too because keeping it hot with the steaks on will also be a challenge.

After heating the Dutch oven pan up for a while, I put the steaks on. The aroma and the sizzle was almost unbearably good. At first, I kept the lid off. In retrospect, I should have kept the lid on because it took a long time to get the meat up to temperature. After 6–7 minutes, I flipped the steaks over and stuck in the thermometer. Like I said, it took a while to get them up to even rare, so I ended up putting the lid on, without coals on top.

When the thermometer read just a little under 140 degrees, I pulled the steaks off and put them on a plate, tented under aluminum foil. Always let meat rest before serving. By the time we were dining, it came up to a nice medium doneness.

In the meantime, I poured the cranberry juice into the same Dutch oven that the steaks had been in. While it sizzled, I used a wooden flipper to scrape up all the fond, the bits of cooked steak and caramelized stuff on the bottom. I had pulled the juice from the fridge, so I think it took a little longer to boil and to start reducing. I whisked the flour and water together, and I added this mixture a little bit at a time to thicken the sauce up. I poured this sauce over the steaks just before serving.

While I was making the sauce, I also put the butter and some of the remaining spice mix into the 8-inch Dutch oven over coals to melt and blend.

Finally, it was all done. We brought it all in and served it up. The seasoned butter was spread on the corn as well as used to dip the crab meat. The pan sauce gave sweetness and tang and blended well with the seasonings and the flavor of the meat. The sweet tones of the corn and the crab also rounded out the otherwise savory-heavy meal. It was a major, four-star feast!

## CHICKEN AND DUMPLINGS

One week, I started flipping through recipe books, looking for something new and challenging. I wanted to try something I'd never done before.

I ended up coming across a cookbook from *The Complete America's Test Kitchen TV Show Cookbook*. I found a recipe for chicken and dumplings and decided I could adapt it for the Dutch oven. Not only had I never cooked it, but I'm not sure that I'd ever eaten it before. I know that's weird. It's about as American as American cuisine gets. But I just don't remember it. So, I was kinda up against something that I was really unfamiliar with.

There are a lot of steps to this process—it's not a simple or basic Dutching dish, but it is a complete one-pot meal: veggies, meat, dairy, and bread all in one. All you need is a glass of iced Diet Dr Pepper and your table is complete! The chicken, of course, makes for a delicious savory tone, but there are lots of smaller bits bringing other tones: the spiciness of the picante, the sweetness of the milk and peas, and the undertones of the dumplings. It really is a well-rounded meal.

### TOOLS

12-inch Dutch oven
Initial steps: 20+ coals below
Final step: about 12–15 coals below, 12–15 coals above

### INGREDIENTS

4 tsp. oil
10–12 chicken thighs
kosher salt
coarse ground black pepper

4–6 green onions
1 jalapeño
4–6 carrots
3–4 stalks celery
2 medium onions
4–6 cloves garlic, minced

juice of 2 lemons (save zest for later use)
6 Tbsp. flour

4–6 cups chicken broth
¼ cup whole milk
1 bag frozen green peas
3 bay leaves
the cooked chicken thighs, shredded or chopped

2 cups unbleached flour
1 Tbsp. baking powder
1 tsp. salt
1 cup whole milk
5–6 Tbsp. reserved chicken fat
zest of 2 lemons
1 tsp. fresh chopped thyme
1 handful fresh chopped parsley

**I STARTED** by firing up some coals and heating some oil in my 12-inch Dutch oven. While that was heating, I opened up the thawed chicken thighs and seasoned them liberally with kosher salt and coarse ground black pepper. You could use chicken breasts, but much of the flavor of this dish comes from the chicken fat that gets rendered out of the thighs.

The first actual cooking step is to put the thighs on the heat and fry them up. I put the lid on because they cook better with the trapped heat. I turned them once during the process and cooked them until they were fully done and the juices ran clear. That was 20 minutes or so.

While they were cooking, I sliced and chopped up all of the ingredients in the second set.

I removed the cooked thighs and put them in a bowl to cool. The recipe book said to remove the skin. I decided not to this time, but in the end, I decided that was a bad choice. Having the skin in the soup wasn't as appetizing as I thought it would be.

I drained off and reserved most of the fat that had been rendered out of the thighs. I added the veggies to what remained in the Dutch oven and cooked them, stirring. I let the veggies brown a bit and then added the lemon juice and scraped up the fond from the bottom of the Dutch oven with a wooden spatula. I added in the flour and stirred it up to coat the veggies in a sort of a semi-roux. While the veggies were cooking, I cut the chicken from the bones and shredded the meat.

Finally, I added the next set of ingredients, the liquids and the chicken, and brought it up to a simmer. While that was heating up, I mixed up the ingredients of the last set for the dumpling dough.

As it approached a boil, I added the herbs and some more salt and pepper to taste. Then I stirred it all up and got the dumpling dough. I dropped it in, a heaping tablespoon at a time, all around the Dutch oven. I put on the lid and then put on the upper coals. (The lower coal number is really just an estimate. Throughout the cooking process, I was adding more coals to the chimney so I'd have a running supply of hot coals.) Once the dumplings were in, I cooked the whole thing for another half hour or so. I only checked it once during the cooking and then again when it was all done.

I was afraid that the dumplings would be soggy. Like I said before, I wasn't sure what to expect. But, in the end, it was delicious. The dumplings swelled up as they cooked, like biscuits do, and the stew was delicious. The dumplings were rich with the savory tones of chicken flavor, from both the stew and the chicken fat added in. There was plenty to share and extra for lunches that week.

## HERB AND BACON CORNISH HEN HALVES

This recipe was pretty cool and easy. A nice, one-pot, one-step meal.

Usually when we buy cornish hens, they're whole, but this time we found some that were split in half down the spine. That made it easy to layer.

### TOOLS

12-inch deep Dutch oven
12–14 coals below
16–18 coals above

### INGREDIENTS

4 medium potatoes
2 medium onions

about 2 Tbsp. olive oil
parsley
basil
oregano
3 cloves garlic, minced
salt
pepper
4 halves of cornish hens (one per person), thawed
4 slices thick-cut bacon

**I STARTED** by creating the bottom layer (I did all this while the coals were heating up). I cut the potatoes into large chunks and the onions into quarters and spread them over the bottom of the Dutch oven. That would serve to elevate the hen halves above the drippings.

Then, I mixed all of the ingredients in the second set for the herb baste. I played it pretty loose with the amounts. Just shake some in the bowl and stir. Taste it and see. I made it a little runnier than a paste.

Make sure that the hens are thawed and pat them dry with paper towels or a clean kitchen towel. I covered a hen half in the herb baste, draped a piece of bacon over it, and set it in the Dutch oven. I had to kind of overlap them a bit to fit them all in. I put the Dutch oven onto the coals until the hens read an internal temperature of 170 degrees.

See? Simple. But delicious.

And afterward, I made poultry stock by boiling the bones. Yum!

## SPICY PUMPKIN SOUP

In the minds of most Americans, it seems, pumpkins and autumn are inseparable. You carve jack-o'-lanterns for your porches on Halloween, and you make pumpkin pie for Thanksgiving. But pumpkins are much more international. They grow them in China, Europe, and even Africa.

Here in America, we buy tons and tons of them, mostly in two forms: the bigger carving pumpkins used for the aforementioned jack-o'-lanterns, and pumpkin pureed in cans. Unfortunately, the carved pumpkins end up rotting in the garbage or smashed on the street. I'm amazed by how much food value is chucked away each year.

Still, this book isn't about crusading; it's about cooking.

Lately, I've been fascinated by the culinary possibilities of the pumpkin. I've done some cool cooking with them in the past. I do my own pumpkin pie, of course. I also love to do a dinner in a pumpkin! You can find the recipes to both of those at marksblackpot.com.

The thing I'm loving more and more about the pumpkin is that it's so adaptable to being the basis for both savory and sweet dishes. And even dishes that combine both elements.

Then, I saw some recipes floating around the Internet for a savory, spicy pumpkin soup. As soon as I saw it, I knew I had to try it. And, of course,

I had to make it my own. So I looked around for some other variations to get some ideas.

To talk about making recipes with pumpkins, you have to understand the difference between certain varieties of pumpkin. The larger pumpkins are made primarily for carving and decorating. They don't taste bad. I've used them in the savory dinner-in-a-pumpkin dish. The smaller ones, however, are much better eatin' punkins. They're often called "pie," "sugar," or "sweet" pumpkins, and that gives you a good idea of why you'd want to cook with them. In addition to being tastier, they're also less stringy. And they're cheaper, 'cuz they're smaller and weigh less.

Also, as Linus taught us many years ago, always select your pumpkins, sweet or otherwise, from the most sincere of pumpkin patches.

Making this soup is a two-part process. First you make the pumpkin puree, then you make the soup. I usually do this over two evenings, but you could do it all in the same day.

## THE PUREE

### TOOLS

12-inch Dutch oven
12–15 coals both above and below

### INGREDIENTS

1 sweet pumpkin
about ½ cup water

**WHEN I** make pumpkin puree, I like to do it as a sort of combination of roasting and steaming. I took one sweet pumpkin that was kind of on the large side and quartered it. That made it pretty easy to scrape out the guts and seeds (which you'll keep for later). I halved those sections lengthwise and, finally, halved them crosswise. I ended up with a bunch of pumpkin triangles, about 3 inches on a side. I put these in a Dutch oven, with water poured in. I put this on the coals. I let it cook for 45–60 minutes. When you can stick a fork in them and feel little or no resistance, they're done.

When they were done, I pulled the wedges off the coals and brought them inside. I separated the cooked flesh from the skin using a spoon and put flesh pieces in my blender. Yes, my electric blender. I've tried, for the sake of Dutch oven authenticity, to do this with a hand blender, and with a potato masher. These all still resulted in a stringy mush. If you want a decent puree, ya gotta plug an electric blender in and fire it up.

In all the times I've done this, I've always put in all of the pumpkins and then run the blender. I think it would be much easier to scoop a few pieces, puree them, and then do a few more. Sometimes it's tough to get the stuff on top to get down to the blades.

The resulting puree went into a zip-top baggie and into the fridge, awaiting the soup the next day!

Also, if you've been following my blog or if you've read any of my previous books, you might notice that this time I didn't sprinkle on the brown sugar like I usually do with the pumpkin pie preparations. Since this is going to be a more savory soup, I thought I'd just cook the pumpkins alone.

I separated the seeds from the goop with my fingers and put the seeds into a colander, where I rinsed and separated them even more. Finally, they were free of orange attachments and no longer slimy, and I spread them out on a cookie sheet to dry. These will figure heavily in our final product in the next step.

## THE SEEDS AND THE SOUP

### TOOLS

12-inch Dutch oven (for the soup)
20–24 coals below

10-inch Dutch oven (for the seeds)
15–20 coals below

12-inch deep Dutch oven (for the pumpkin bowls)
12–15 coals below
12–15 coals above

### INGREDIENTS

4 Tbsp. unsalted butter
2 medium yellow onions
4 cloves garlic
2 cups cooked and shredded chicken

2 Tbsp. oil
dried pumpkin seeds
liberal shakes of seasoning salt or other spice blend

¼ tsp. crushed red pepper
½ tsp. ground cumin

pinch of ground cayenne pepper
salt
pepper

2 sweet pumpkins

6 cups pumpkin puree (that I made the night before)
1 cup milk
3–5 cups chicken broth
1–2 Tbsp. corn masa
½ cup water

sour cream
chopped fresh parsley

**I STARTED** by lighting up a lot of coals. This one took a while to do, so I went through quite a few coals over time. At one point, I had three Dutch ovens going at once.

I put the standard 12-inch oven over some coals and started melting the butter. I diced up the onions and minced the garlic. I also cut the chicken (which was already pulled from the birds I roasted up the previous week) into smaller bits. By the way, if you have more or less chicken, it's fine. In fact, it would be a great soup without it. I put it in because I thought it would add a little more substance and texture to the dish.

I also put the 10-inch on some coals, with some oil in the bottom, to heat up.

Once the Dutch ovens were heated up, I tossed the onions and the garlic into the 12-inch and the pumpkin seeds into the 10-inch. Both got stirred up. I added the seasoning salt to the seeds. I also put the lid on the seeds, to trap the heat. I stirred both the seeds and the onions frequently.

After the onions were getting translucent, I added the chicken. I let that sizzle and brown for a little bit and then added the spices. I would recommend that you add the spices light at this stage, and then boost them as the overall soup is simmering if you want it to be hotter. It's easy to add heat. It's impossible to take it out. As it turned out, I really liked the level of heat I got.

Somewhere around here, the pumpkin seeds were turning nice and brown and crispy. I took them off the coals but left them in the Dutch oven. There's a point when cooking pumpkin seeds when they become a little too brown and almost burnt. They start to smoke a little bit. Personally, I love that flavor!

I snapped off the stems of the two pumpkins and sliced them open across the "equator." I scooped out all the guts and scraped out the stringy bits and put the four halves in the 12-inch deep Dutch oven with a bit of water in the bottom. I had to kind of snuggle them in there. I put that on the coals and let them roast/steam/cook.

I got a big mixing bowl and dumped in the pumpkin puree. Then I poured in the milk and stirred it up. I added 2 cups of the chicken broth, and, while stirring, I kept adding more broth until it was just a bit runnier than I wanted the final soup to be. Once I got to the consistency I was looking for, I added that to the Dutch oven with the chicken and onions. I let it get back up to temperature and then adjusted the coals to get a consistent simmer going on, uncovered.

At that point, the busy work ends and the relaxing part begins. All you have to do is stir and taste the soup, check the pumpkins, and keep the coals fresh and hot. The pumpkins will probably take 45–60 minutes to cook. As the soup simmers along, you can adjust the consistency as you like. Add more broth if it's too thick. Mix the corn masa and the water, and add drizzles of it to the soup if it's too runny. Add more cayenne if it's too weak or more salt to bring out all the other flavors. You really get to choose the tones of your soup. The pumpkin brings the sweet, the chicken and broth bring the savory, and the spices bring a bit of heat.

When the pumpkins are done, and the soup is satisfactory, then you get to assemble them and serve them. This was the most fun part of all,

because after all of that two-day work, it all comes together here.

I put the cooked pumpkin bowls in regular bowls and filled them up to brimming with soup. Then, I added a small spoonful of sour cream right in the middle of both pumpkin bowls. I sprinkled the roasted pumpkin seeds all around, and finished it off with a sprinkle of chopped fresh parsley. If you cooked the pumpkin seeds right, they'll bring that smoky bitter tone that will really make this dish great.

Then, we sat down to eat. The soup itself was tasty and spicy. Occasionally, I'd get a bite with a seed, and the smokey-roasted flavor would set of a whole new taste. It also added a crunchy texture to an otherwise completely soft dish. I would scrape a bit of the "bowl" into some bites of the soup too for added pumpkin goodness.

A five-star meal if there ever was one!

## BERRIED CHICKEN

My first encounter with combining fruit and poultry was at a sandwich shop that sold a turkey sandwich with raspberry jam. I was skeptical, but my wife raved about it, so I tried it. In a single bite, I was convinced. Yum!

I saw this recipe for raspberry-baked chicken over at Dutch Oven Madness (dutchovenmadness.blogspot.com), and it really intrigued me. She said she didn't like her result, however, and I wasn't sure why at first. The recipe drew me in, however, and made me want to experiment with it. I thought that one of the reasons why it might not have had a good flavor, as she said, was that all there was to it was chicken and sweet. I thought that there needed to be some savory flavors to add a bit to the chicken; then the sweet and tang of the berries would be another layer of flavor. I did some Web research and got some ideas of how to expand it. A couple of recipes used some spices and the berries as a marinade. That sounded kinda interesting.

My first results were good, but not great. I liked the taste, and so did my friends, but it didn't look as great as I'd hoped. I cooked it all together, and the berry marinade ended up as a purple-brown soupy sauce. I also wasn't blown away by it. My friends all had seconds, so that was a good sign. But it wasn't as "wow" as I'd hoped.

I thought I could do better. Instead of adding all the ingredients to the marinade and cooking the chicken, I thought to make the chicken separate from the berry sauce and then serve them together. I think that would make the savory and the sweet tones more distinct. Another thing to do differently is to make sure that the chicken is fully thawed and patted dry. There was a lot of liquid still in the chicken, and so the berry sauce ended up too runny that first time, and I had to thicken it with some cornstarch. I was hoping it would be more of a glaze, and that didn't work.

So I tried it again, and this one worked! I was very excited by the look and taste of the result.

Plus, it sounds so cool to tell people, "I'm cooking berried chicken tonight!" I get lots of strange looks.

**TOOLS**
12-inch Dutch oven
10 coals below
14 coals above

10-inch Dutch oven
12–14 coals below

**INGREDIENTS**
3–4 lbs. chicken breast (I used frozen)

### THE SPICE RUB
about 1 Tbsp. olive oil
about 1 Tbsp. kosher salt
about 1 Tbsp. pepper
about 1 Tbsp. paprika
about 1 tsp. dry mustard
about 1 tsp. chili powder
about 2 tsp. garlic powder

3–4 medium potatoes, quartered and chunked

1 cup blueberries, plus some extra
1 cup raspberries, plus some extra
1 cup blackberries, plus some extra
½ of a 12-oz. can apple juice concentrate
2–3 Tbsp. fresh chopped mint
cinnamon

**I STARTED** with the chicken meat. Since I used frozen chicken pieces, I'd recommend thawing them completely, draining them, and patting them dry in paper towels. Then, I mixed up the spice ingredients. When I did this, I was guessing at amounts. I was basically creating a rub, so you could even use a prepackaged meat/grilling seasoning. I kept mixing at about these proportions, tasting it along the way. If you want more of one thing or another, you can adjust it.

Then, I shook the rub liberally over the meat and put it all in the fridge for a few hours.

I got the coals ready and gave my Dutch oven a quick spritz of spray oil. Then I scattered the potatoes over the bottom of the oven and layered the chicken on top of those. The potatoes let the chicken drain its juices and absorbed much of the flavor from that and the spice rub. I put that on the coals to bake.

Toni, over at Dutch Oven Madness, just used raspberries. I used a mix of berries because the first store I visited didn't have any raspberries. I did finally find some, though, so I just decided to mix it all in. I added most of the berries and the juice concentrate into a bowl and mashed it all up together. I saved some of each kind of berry, whole, to add into the sauce later.

At this point, I put the berry mix alone into my 10-inch Dutch oven and put it on the coals to simmer and reduce.

As the chicken neared done and the sauce was good and thick, I stirred some full, raw berries into the sauce so they'd have enough time to come up to temperature (but not really "cook") before serving over the baked and seasoned chicken. As an afterthought, I added some chopped fresh mint leaves, for a bit of a cool tone, and a few shakes of cinnamon to give it some edge and even enhance the sweet tones.

The end result was stunning. It's one of the best things I think I've ever cooked. The sweet of the berries blended beautifully with the spice of the chicken. The berries even mellowed the over-spiciness a bit. Not cooking them together was a smart move. The two flavor blends were much more distinct this way, yet they still combined.

My family, however, wasn't as impressed as I was. They weren't unimpressed, either, but my son was a bit nervous to try the berry sauce. And even though my wife liked the berries, she loved the chicken plain and was scarfing down the potatoes like there was no tomorrow.

So, many thanks to Toni for the inspiration and the motivation to try something new! To experiment! That's what helps me to learn.

# Foods I Hated

In 1990, President George Bush raised up a big row by declaring to the world that he hated broccoli. He said, in essence, that he'd always hated it as a child. His mom had told him that if he got to be president of the United States, he could decide not to eat broccoli. But as a child, he'd have to eat it. Since he was the president, he wasn't going to eat it any more.

Angry broccoli growers descended on Washington and stood on the sidewalk throwing florets onto the White House Lawn. The press had a field day with it. I'm not making this up.

There were actually quite a few foods that I grew up hating. Broccoli was one. Squash was another. My mom is actually an excellent cook. But this was one dish she served up that was horror on a plate. Her squash was this boiled, pureed glop of orange, and it tasted gross and had a texture that was like melted modeling clay. Liver was another one I couldn't stand. Asparagus and I were bitter enemies. I loathed the slimy sticks of bitterness. They could fill my soul with ugliness like no other vegetables could. I hated them so much that one day I was possessed to actually trample my mother's asparagus patch. Many years later she and I could laugh about it. Not on that day, however.

Mom and Dad devised a deal, which they offered to us kids. We could pick one food, one item that for the whole next year, we didn't have to eat. No matter how often it was cooked for us, we didn't have to touch it. The tradeoff, however, was that we were obliged to eat everything else with dignified and calm acceptance.

I almost always chose asparagus. And I have a hard time believing that I ate everything else with dignity and calmness.

Why am I bringing this up? There comes a point in everyone's life where we just have to grow up. Mine occurred a little late in life, I guess. I wrote about it in my blog:

> Well, the last week or so I've been contemplating my now-annual Mother's Day feast. I've been thinking about what to cook for it. For the meat/main dish, I've been seriously considering a pork crown roast. I mean, for sheer "wow," there's not much that will beat a crown roast. And in one of my Dutch oven cookbooks, there's a recipe for one with this mushroom and asparagus side dish.

Everything looks just great, except for those blasted asparagus.

But, you know, when it comes to making a plate look high-class, there are few veggies that will dress it up like asparagus.

But can I do it?

Over the years, I've managed to make peace with broccoli. I don't mind it, now. I still don't like liver and squash. Sweet potatoes, not so much, either.

Everyone tells me that good asparagus relies on the method of cooking. But see, my mom was a great cook, and I have a hard time believing she'd done it wrong all those years. I mean, Dad loved it, and even my sister grew to love it. What's wrong with me?

So could I swallow my pride and swallow the asparagus?

A week or so later, I posted this:

### ALERT THE MEDIA

Okay.

I did it.

I did the deed.

I am forever changed.

I went to Smith's Grocery Store. I walked in. And I actually paid my own good, hard-earned money for a bundle of asparagus. What is this world coming to?!

Pleeeeease, please, don't tell my mom!

And the following week, I cooked it.

Yes, I did it. I cooked asparagus, and I even liked it. Yes, there, I admitted it. I even called Mom and told her and Dad about it. They thought that was pretty funny. Dad said I was finally growing up.

## SALMON WITH POTATOES AND ASPARAGUS

To make this dish, I used my "dry-roasting" cooking technique. I first tried it when I did the Jerk Chicken (see page 117) and again when I did the Pseudo-Indian Chicken (see page 138). The basic idea is that a Dutch oven usually cooks by trapping the steam and the heat. The heavy lid traps all the moisture in. That's great with almost everything you cook, but once in a while, you want to cook something that's a bit more dry.

To make it work, you put something under the lid to lift it up. I found a thin metal grill that I could place under the lid. It lifted the lid, but not much. That way, the moisture escaped. When I first tried this, I found, however, that a lot of the heat did too.

So, in order to make it work, you have to up the lid coals *significantly.* I put a thermometer in the bottom of the Dutch oven while I was cooking the potatoes and found that I needed to almost double the coals in order to get the kind of heat needed. I liked the results of cooking that way. It does lose a lot of heat that would have normally been trapped, however.

**TOOLS**
12-inch Dutch oven
in the dry-roasting phase: 25+ coals each above and below
in the final baking phase: 10–12 coals below, 18–20 coals above.

**INGREDIENTS**
4–5 medium to large potatoes
olive oil
parsley
salt
pepper
1–2 cloves garlic, minced

oil

fresh asparagus, about 4–5 sprigs per serving
olive oil
salt
lemon pepper or lemon zest and pepper

1 fresh salmon fillet
dill
1 bundle green onions, chopped
1 lemon, sliced

**I STARTED** by lighting up the fire. That was a bit of a challenge as windy as it was, but eventually I had coals getting white. While those got ready, I got to cleaning the potatoes. The original recipe I adapted this from called for baby potatoes. That would have been yummy, but I didn't have any, so I used regular potatoes, quartered and then sliced into cube-like chunks.

I put them in a bowl and dashed over some olive oil followed by all of the other seasonings and flavorings. I shook the bowl and mixed them all up.

Then I went out and put the oven on the coals to preheat. I spritzed a little extra oil in the bottom. I don't know that I needed to, but I did. Once the oven was a bit hot, I put in the potatoes. I let those cook for a while, using the dry-roasting technique described on the previous page, until they got good and seared on all sides and the seasonings were clinging to them. Since I was playing with the temperature, it took a little longer, but I think in normal conditions it should take about 30 minutes or so, with a couple of stirrings.

While that was happening, I was preparing the asparagus and the salmon.

The asparagus was easy enough. I cut off about the bottom third of the asparagus because I remembered the bottom being the nastiest part when I was a kid. I put the sprigs into a bag with just a splash of oil and the salt and lemon stuff. I didn't have any lemons that day, so I just used lemon pepper. I shook it up to coat the asparagus sprigs.

Then I cut the salmon fillet into four big pieces (that's how many we would be eating). I sprinkled on the dill, scattered over the chopped green onions, and put a lemon slice on each one.

I took all that out to the ovens. I took off the lid and the grill separator and added the asparagus to the now delicious-looking potatoes and stirred them together. I laid the salmon fillet pieces in on top of those and put the lid on solid. I readjusted the coals and began baking the salmon and asparagus with the potatoes.

Because it's still quite hot, it didn't take long to cook the salmon, maybe 15–20 more minutes. At that point the asparagus was al dente. It was definitely cooked, but it wasn't wilted. It was still a bit crunchy, resisting my teeth a bit. The oil had kept the seasonings tight to the stalks and tight to the potatoes, so those were quite yummy, and the salmon was delicious too.

This meal really turned out four-star, if I do say so myself. The bitter tones of the asparagus were not harsh, and the savory tones of the spices and the fish (which also had some subtle sweetness) made for a great overall dish.

Yeah, growing up can be worth it.

# The Seafood Feast, Part 1: Smoking Salmon

A long time ago, I was surfin' the Internet looking for some Dutch oven ideas, and I came across outdoorcooking.com. One of the blog postings was all about smoking salmon in a Dutch oven. When I first saw that I had one of those sit-back-and-slap-your-forehead moments. I knew that someday I would try it.

One weekend, I did. In fact, I tried a couple of seafood dishes that had been stacking up in my queue. Now, not only was I trying out two dishes that I had never before tried, I was also trying a technique I had never even seen before. Add to this that the other dish was mussels, which I had no experience with either, and my confusion and stress levels were high enough.

Then, to make matters worse, I invited my neighbors over! What was I thinking? Haven't I said before, "Never cook a first-time dish for friends"? Yeah, well, I don't take my own advice either. These friends are used to being my guinea pigs anyway.

Back to the outdoor cooking blog: I liked this guy's idea for putting the smoking chips under aluminum foil and a grill. *But what if*, I thought, *I need to add more chips?* This was my idea: Inside a larger Dutch oven, put a smaller Dutch oven lid, inverted, on a lid stand. Chips go below, salmon on the lid, larger lid on top, propped open . . . *Boom*. Dutch oven smoker.

But I had no idea if it would work. Would it get hot enough to smolder the chips? Would it be too hot so as to fast-cook the salmon? I had no idea.

Ah, such is the adventure!

## SMOKED SALMON

### TOOLS

14-inch deep Dutch oven
40+ coals below

10-inch Dutch oven lid, with a lid stand

### INGREDIENTS

smoking chips of your favorite flavor

1 big salmon piece, about 8 oz. per serving (I did about 7)

salt
pepper
any herbs you like (I used thyme and sage)
1 lemon, sliced

**I STARTED** by lighting up some coals. I wanted to try out the setup before I actually put the salmon on to see if it would smoke. I put the 14-inch on a monstrous boatload of coals. I gave a rough count, and it was about 45. I scattered a layer of dry smoking chips (I used applewood) on the bottom. I put an oven thermometer on top of that. I wanted to be able to monitor things.

I have a bent piece of wire, about 1/8 of an inch in diameter. I hooked that over the edge and put the lid on. That raised the lid enough to vent. I set that aside and checked the temperature from time to time.

In the meantime, I prepared the salmon. I trimmed off the skin and shook some salt, pepper, and herbs on each piece, both sides. I left that to sit.

It took a while to heat up the Dutch oven, but once it did, I was pleased to see smoke pouring out when I went to check it. The interior temperature was about 250 degrees, which was perfect for smoking. I put the lid stand in the middle of the Dutch oven and put the lid on the stand, inverted. I put the salmon on the resultant platform. I put round slices of lemon on the salmon and set the lid back on. Just to be sure I did it right, I put a short-stemmed meat thermometer in one of the thicker parts of salmon. I also left the oven thermometer in.

From that point on, I just checked the smoke, the temperatures, and the salmon every 30–40 minutes. It fluctuated as high as 350 degrees and as low as 200. I tried to keep it lower. I did add coals, but after a while, I found it wasn't as necessary to keep as many on to maintain good temperatures or smoke. I did add some chips at one point because I saw it not smoking as much. I just sprinkled them in through the gap between the lid and the wall of the Dutch oven.

Finally, after about 2 hours, the meat temperature read about 170 degrees. It was done! And I served it up on the rice (in the following recipe).

## The Seafood Feast, Part 2: Dutch Oven Mussels

For a long time now, my family has frequented a certain Asian buffet house. They have great food, and the people who run it are wonderful. We love their more traditional Chinese dishes, and we also love their sushi. My son Brendon particularly likes their unagi.

They have one dish that I love that I had vowed to attempt. I don't know just how authentically Chinese it is, but I love the taste! I also vowed that when I attempted it, I would not duplicate it but would rather explore it on my own. In the end, I think it had a more American taste to it, so I'm including it here.

It is a mussel cooked in its own half-shell, with a layering of cream cheese and a sprinkling of cheddar on top. I did some research and found out a lot about cooking and working with mussels. I cooked this the same day as the smoked salmon of the previous recipe. It was a bit tricky working both dishes at the same time, but in the end they really complemented each other.

## THREE-CHEESE BAKED MUSSELS

### TOOLS
12-inch Dutch oven
for steaming: 22+ coals below
for baking: 8–10 coals below, 18–20 coals above

### INGREDIENTS
2 (8-oz.) bricks cream cheese
2–3 Tbsp. sun-dried tomatoes
Parmesan cheese
herbs (I used thyme and rosemary)
chives
salt
lemon zest
grated cheddar cheese
chili powder

3–4 lbs. live mussels
1 cup water
½ cup apple cider vinegar

1 cup grated cheddar cheese

## THE RICE

### TOOLS
8-inch Dutch oven
10–12 coals below

### INGREDIENTS
juice of 1 lemon
1 cup long-grain rice
2 cups liquid (from the mussels; add water as needed)

**BECAUSE THERE** would be relatively little downtime once the cooking got started, the first step was to prepare the cheese topping. I added all the ingredients in the first set together and mixed it up with a fork.

I don't really remember the exact amounts of each flavoring item. I added things at the top of the list in slightly greater quantities than the things at the bottom (chili powder being the least of all), but really, I just mixed it all and tasted it as I went. While I did add some cheddar to the overall mix, I didn't add much, as I knew that more would be sprinkled on top later.

The coals were already started for the salmon, so I didn't have to get anything set aside special for this dish. I just had to make sure that there were enough coals getting white. While that was happening, I started to clean the mussels. I got them into my sink and scrubbed each one down, on both sides of the shell, with a plastic brush. Many of them had a little stringy substance dangling out between the two shell halves. This is called the "beard," and I scraped that off with a knife.

I'd read to remove those mussels that were opened. The instructions said that those were dead already. That's a little tricky to say because there were quite a few that were slightly opened that would close up again after we had separated them out. I guess those ones weren't so dead. There were many, however, that were clearly open and clearly dead. I removed those.

There were a lot of them to clean. About halfway through the process, I added the water and the cider in the bottom of the 12-inch Dutch oven, and I got that started on the coals, covered. I wanted to get it boiling.

By the time I was completely finished cleaning all the mussels, it was boiling. I unceremoniously dumped them all in, stirred them up a bit, and closed the lid. It didn't take long, maybe ten minutes, to steam them open. I'd read that you shouldn't overcook them, especially at this stage.

I took them off the coals and drained them in a colander, retaining all the liquid for the rice.

I began the process of assembling the half shells. Here's how it went:

- First, I pulled the shells open. Usually, one of the shells (the "top") was free of meat, and the other (the "bottom") held the mussel. I broke them apart and discarded the top.
- Then, I took a knife and ran it under the meat, cutting the attachment between it and the shell. There's one spot where it clings pretty tight, and it makes it much easier to eat if that's severed. Still, I kept the meat in the shell bottom.
- Next, I spread a bit of the cheese mix onto the shell and over the meat. Not too much; it's not there to smother the meat, but to complement it.
- Finally, I placed the shell into the bottom of the 12-inch Dutch oven. I kept repeating this whole process until they were all done. There were a lot of shells, so I had to pack them in pretty tight.

- Finally, finally, I sprinkled on a layer of grated cheddar.

I put on the lid and arranged the coals under and on top to bake.

I also took some time during the prep time to set the rice. I measured the liquid I had drained off the mussels after the steaming. I had read that the mussels would release a lot of their own liquid as they cooked and that would be a good flavoring broth. That, combined with the water, the cider, and the lemon juice, and I had just under 2 cups. A little more water topped it right off. This, along with 1 cup of rice, went onto the coals to cook.

A little bit after I had set the mussels on to bake, I could see the steam venting from under the lid of the 8-inch Dutch oven. I let it go for about 5 more minutes and then pulled it off the coals to finish steaming in its own residual heat. Don't take off the lid to check it!

The mussels in the 12-inch Dutch oven didn't bake long. You don't want to overcook the meat. You just want to heat up the cheese mixture and melt the cheddar on top. I let it go 10–20 minutes from the time I put it on.

I served it up with a few mussels on the plate, next to a bed of the rice, with a big cut of smoked salmon atop the bed. It looked and tasted delicious, and I felt like I had really accomplished something. I had done two dishes, one with a new technique and another with a new main ingredient, and they were both successes. That's a good, good feeling!

# Southwestern

The Dutch oven is closely tied to the history of the American West and to the legacy of the pioneers, the mountain men, the explorers, and the cowboys of the cattle drives. All their recipes, with heavy influence from nearby Mexico, make for a rich and hearty cuisine! In recent years, it has grown from its roots as food for the working poor to the doors of fancy restaurants.

Personally, I love it all!

## SPICY ROAST CHICKEN

I did something similar a few months prior to this on a turkey, and it was phenomenal. My whole family loved it. It's a simple dish. It only takes a few minutes and a few ingredients to prepare it (once the chicken itself is thawed). All you do is prepare a rub (more of a spice and flavoring paste, really) and cover the chicken in it. It is basic, simple Dutching at its finest. Of course, the results taste far from basic. That's the beauty of it!

I'm particularly proud of this one, because even though it's based on some things that are pretty common, like basic jerk chicken, it's my own combination.

**TOOLS**

12-inch deep Dutch oven
14–15 coals above and below

**INGREDIENTS**

1 (5–7 lb.) chicken
1 onion, sliced
4–5 green onions, sliced

½ Tbsp. cayenne pepper
½ Tbsp. paprika
½ Tbsp. salt
½ Tbsp. pepper
½ Tbsp. cumin powder
½ cup chopped fresh cilantro
4–5 green onions, sliced
zest of 1 lemon
juice of 1 lemon
olive oil

**OKAY, HERE'S** how you do it. Follow these steps and you'll really wow them.

First, I thawed the chicken and patted it dry. One thing I like to do with poultry is to take a fork or sharp knife and poke holes in the skin to allow more of the spice flavor to seep into the meat. I put the chicken, breast-side up, in the bottom of the deep Dutch oven. I don't know if it would have fit in a shallow. I didn't check, to be honest.

Then I took the onions and the green onions and scattered them around the sides of the chicken.

While the coals were getting hot, I took a little time to make the spice rub/paste. It's simple to do. I mixed all the ingredients in the second set except the oil. You can adjust them to taste. If you like yours to be a little spicier, with more bite, add more cayenne and so on. Do it how you like it, or follow what I've got here.

Once those ingredients are all mixed in and stirred up, I gradually added a bit of oil while stirring—just enough to make it like a paste.

I took a fork and smeared that paste all over the top surfaces of the chicken. I covered as much as I could, but I didn't want it to end up on the bottom of the Dutch oven.

Then I put it on the coals. You have to keep a side fire going for some extra coals. The ones I started with on my Dutch oven went out long before the chicken was done. So about every 20 minutes or so, I added another 5–10 coals into the side fire. These catch fire from the ones that were in there, still burning before. About 20 minutes later, I pulled some out to supplement those that were now burning out. Doing this, I was able to keep the heat on almost indefinitely.

This chicken took about 1½ hours to reach the internal temperature of about 180 degrees. (I used a thermometer stuck in the breast. It's the easiest way to tell if it's done.)

Since it's done in the Dutch oven, it comes out moist and steamed. The spices seep down in, and man, it's great! Probably my favorite roast chicken recipe ever!

## Cajun

In the 1700s, French settlers lived in what is now Nova Scotia and Quebec, which they called "Acadia." They refused allegiance to Britain after the French and Indian War. They were expelled and traveled by boat to Haiti and then to Louisiana, where they were called "Acadians." If you pronounce the "dian" with a "j" sound, you can see where the name "Cajuns" came from. They are now recognized as a unique sub-ethnic group.

And I love their food!

### ZESTY JAMBALAYA

This is a cool jambalaya that I pulled from various sources on the Internet. Here it is with my adaptations and commentary.

#### TOOLS

12-inch Dutch oven
15–18 coals below

**INGREDIENTS**
2 Tbsp. olive oil
1 tsp. minced garlic
1 onion, chopped
1 green bell pepper, chopped
2 long stalks of celery, chopped
1 lb. smoked sausage, sliced thin
1 (14.5-oz.) can diced tomatoes, undrained
1 heaping tsp. salt
½ tsp. dried thyme
⅓ tsp. crushed red pepper
1 bay leaf
liberal shaking of cajun spice mix
1½ cups chicken broth
1 cup uncooked rice

**FIRST, I** heated the Dutch oven with some oil in the bottom. It was a 12-inch shallow oven (my workhorse), and I had 15–18 coals on the bottom. Then I put in the garlic and the veggies. I stirred that around a bit until I saw some brown, especially in the garlic. Then I put in the sausage and stirred that in. I cooked it for a while, until it had a nice caramelized brown to it.

Then I added the tomatoes and the spices, along with the chicken broth. I let that simmer for about 20 minutes, covered.

Then I added the rice, covered it up, and let it simmer. I took a lot of the underneath coals and put them on the top. I probably had 10–12 below, and the same on top. I let it simmer for 30–40 minutes, until I felt the rice was done. I served it up, and it was yummy!

Here's a variation:

## SALMON AND JAMBALAYA

**TOOLS**
12-inch Dutch oven
10–12 coals both above and below

**INGREDIENTS**
all the ingredients for the previous jambalaya, plus

4–6 (8-oz.) salmon filets
cajun spice mix
butter
lemon

**THIS ONE** is a variation of the previous Jambalaya recipe, combined with the lemon salmon recipe I did for my folks and at the cook-off years ago. It turned out *really* well.

I started off just making the jambalaya according to the recipe. When I put the broth, tomatoes, and so on into the Dutch oven, I also set the salmon on top. I dusted them liberally with a really great cajun spice mix and then topped that with a slice of butter and a slice of lemon, just like the other salmon recipe.

I left it to simmer, cooking the rice and the salmon. It was a yummy and tangy dinner.

## BLACKENED SALMON ON VEGGIE RICE

One year, I had been struggling with what to cook at the Eagle Mountain Pony Express Days Cook-Off. I'd finally settled on some dishes and did a trial run. The cook-off required three dishes: a bread, an entrée, and a dessert. I decided on the braided bread with an orange and brown sugar glaze, a blackened salmon on a bed of rice and veggies, and the paradise pie knockoff recipe I had done months before. I had to work out a schedule that was pretty tight in order to deliver the three dishes on time.

But here, right now, I'm going to share the salmon and rice.

### TOOLS

2 (12-inch) Dutch ovens
20+ coals beneath each one

### INGREDIENTS

**The Salmon**

1 Tbsp. cumin
1 Tbsp. crushed coriander
1 Tbsp. garlic powder
1 Tbsp. coarse ground black pepper
1 Tbsp. thyme
2 Tbsp. paprika
2 Tbsp. salt
1 tsp. oregano
4–6 salmon fillets

**The Veggie Rice**

2 sweet peppers (I used half each of red, yellow, orange, and green, for color)
1 jalapeño

4 green onions
1 onion, sliced
2 Tbsp. minced garlic
¼ lb. smoked sausage, thinly sliced
1 cup rice
2 cups chicken stock
zest of 1 lemon
juice of 2 lemons
salt and pepper

**FIRST, I** mixed all the spices in the first set of ingredients in a zip-top bag. Then I cut the skin away from the salmon fillets and cut them into chunks about two inches wide. I put the fillets into the bag, closed it, and shook it all up to really coat the salmon. Then I pulled the salmon out, shook off the excess spice (an important step), and put them into another bag, letting them sit and absorb the spices for about an hour.

Then I chopped up the sweet peppers, jalapeño, and green onions. I put the onions, garlic, and sausage on the coals to brown. Once those were ready, I put in the rest of the veggies, the rice, and the stock. Then I added the lemon zest and juice and the salt and pepper. I covered the Dutch oven and left it on the coals (I transferred some to the top) for about 20 minutes, until the rice was done.

While the rice was cooking, I finished the salmon. I put a lot of coals under another 12-inch oven with just a few tablespoons of oil in the bottom, and I put the lid on. I let it heat up a lot. Then I took the salmon fillets and put them into the oil and let them sizzle for about 2 minutes before I turned them over. The seasoning was good and black, and man, it smelled great! After another two minutes, I pulled the Dutch oven off the coals, covered it with the Dutch oven lid, and let the residual heat cook the fish the rest of the way through.

You can serve it up how you like, but I laid down a bed of rice and then set the blackened salmon on top. It tasted great. The salmon had a slightly sweet tone underneath all of the savory spices. The rice was also savory, but the undertone of the rice was nice too.

## CRAYFISH BOIL

Recently, we had one of the most amazing, fun, and delicious family experiences in a long time. We went crawdad catching and then had a Cajun crayfish boil and feast.

Let me interject here that I don't really know what to call them: Crawdads? Crawfish? Crayfish? Mud bugs? Lil' lobster mini-me's? I think "crayfish" sounds more dignified and "crawdad" sounds more bayou. My kids liked the sound of "crawdad" better, so that's what we ended up calling them.

Then I faced another difficult problem. Not only did I not know what to call them, I also didn't know how to cook them! I surfed all over the Net looking for advice and recipes. There were plenty of suggestions. Too many, in fact. Too much contradiction. Everyone said that their way of doing it was the only way of doing it.

Normally when I encounter that, I just brush it all off as folklore and do a kind of hybrid of everyone's recipes. But the contradictory information was more of the type that scared me. "If you do it this way or that way, then your crayfish will die, and you don't *ever* eat crayfish that died before you killed them!" "Don't do this, don't do that!" It was all quite frustrating and confusing. In the end, though, it all worked out.

**TOOLS**

2 (14-inch) deep Dutch ovens
a whopping *lot* of coals underneath each (I'd estimate it was between 30–40 coals under each oven)

**INGREDIENTS**

15–20 lbs. live crayfish
1 carton salt
a lot of water to rinse the crayfish

1 Tbsp. black pepper
1 Tbsp. coriander
1½ Tbsp. cloves
1½ Tbsp. allspice
¼ lb. kosher salt
3 Tbsp. cayenne pepper
2 Tbsp. garlic powder
1 Tbsp. thyme
1 Tbsp. oregano
1 Tbsp. dry mustard
6 bay leaves, crushed
enough water to fill the Dutch oven to about ¾ full
4 onions, sliced
2 heads garlic, broken apart, not peeled
3 jalapeños, sliced
3 lbs. potatoes, chopped into 1-inch sections
8 ears corn, broken in half
1 lb. sausage (andouille or smoked), cut into ½-inch pieces

**I WON'T** go into the catching. That will be for another time. Here we'll just talk about the cooking. I started with the crayfish. The first thing I did was "purge" them. The idea is to make them sick so they purge out their guts before you try to eat them. I filled up the cooler where I had them stored with water and shook in about ½ carton of salt. Right away, the crayfish reacted, swimming and thrashing around in the water.

I drained the cooler and then repeated the process. At the time, I was nervous about killing them, but it turns out that you have to try *really hard* to kill them. Like, dropping them in seasoned, boiling water. Salt may freak them out, but it doesn't kill them. Yet.

I filled the cooler up again, and drained it again, this time without salt. I repeated that clean rinsing process again. Next time, I'm going to do that many, many more times to clean them more thoroughly.

While I was doing the "salt, rinse, repeat" thing, I also got out the Dutch ovens and started up the coals. Once the coals were basically hot, I put the Dutch ovens on and filled them about ¾ of the way with water. I put the lids on, because water boils better in Dutch ovens that way. I also knew that it was going to take a long time to boil that much water.

I mixed up the spices and began cutting the veggies while I waited for the water to boil. The spices I split in half, and put half in each Dutch oven. I put one head of garlic (broken up) and two sliced onions into each pot.

I kept the coals replenished and as hot as could be. Once the water was boiling, I put in the potatoes, sausage, and corn. As soon as I did that, of course, it stopped boiling. I put the lids back on and let it come back up to a good steady boil. I let it cook until the potatoes were almost soft enough to eat, and the corn looked bright yellow.

Finally came the moment we'd all been waiting for. Using my food tongs, I started grabbing the crayfish and dropping them into the boiling pots. I tried to keep them even between the two. I don't know that it mattered a whole lot, though. They turned this rich red-brown color almost immediately. I put the lids back on and let them come back up to a boil for a little bit, mostly to give the spices time to infuse in the meat. Finally, I used a strainer to scoop out the crayfish and the corn, potatoes, and sausage.

Traditionally, you serve crayfish poured directly onto a newspaper-covered tabletop. We actually used dishes.

After only a few, I got the hang of eating them. I would grab the crayfish tightly between the tail and the shell and twist the tail off. I would pinch pretty hard, so as to not get so much of the guts in the body. Then, I'd crack off the first one or two segments of shell on the tail. Gripping the end of the tail between my thumb and forefinger, I squeezed while tugging the meat out with my teeth. I never built up the courage to suck out the head, like some people do. There's not much meat in the tail. That's why you cook up so many of them!

After every few crayfish, I'd pause and eat a few potatoes, onions, or corn cobs. Oh, and the sausage. Those were all delicious. It was the first time I'd tasted corn that sweet and spicy!

Even though it all tasted delicious, at the end of it all, this was not so much a dish to cook as it was a whole experience for the family to savor. It was one that we'll remember for a very long time!

## PENNE ALFREDO WITH BLACKENED CAJUN CHICKEN

Back when I was working on a chapter on herbs, spices, and flavorings for my book *Black Pot for Beginners*, I wanted to test out the Cajun blackening mix on chicken, instead of salmon, like I had done a few years ago. I wasn't quite sure what to do with it, though. What to serve it with? Rice? Potatoes? Those both sounded good, but in the end I decided on penne pasta with an Alfredo sauce.

It turned out to be both complex and simple. It's simple in that it only took about an hour to an hour and a half to do the entire meal (not counting the thaw time for the chicken) and that no single part was complicated. However, I was cooking three things at once—the chicken, the pasta, and the Alfredo sauce. It was tricky to balance them all to be done at about the same time.

First, I mixed up the blackening powder mix. I would recommend doing a double or triple batch and storing the excess in an old spice bottle. Make sure you label it, or you'll look at it in three months and say, "What on earth is this stuff?"

### MARK'S BLACKENING MIX

#### INGREDIENTS

Mix together:

- 2 tsp. cumin

2 tsp. crushed coriander
2 tsp. garlic powder
2 tsp. coarse ground black pepper
2 tsp. thyme
3 tsp. paprika
3 tsp. salt
1 tsp. oregano
½ tsp. cayenne pepper

## THE PASTA

### TOOLS
10-inch Dutch oven
20+ coals below

### INGREDIENTS
some water (enough to almost fill the Dutch oven)
1 lb. penne pasta (or any kind of pasta you like)

## MARK'S BLACKENED CHICKEN

### TOOLS
12-inch Dutch oven
24+ coals below to start, then
12–14 coals below
13–15 coals above

### INGREDIENTS
4 boneless, skinless chicken breasts
Mark's Blackening Mix (above)
spray oil
1–2 Tbsp. olive oil

## THE ALFREDO SAUCE

### TOOLS
8-inch Dutch oven
10+ coals below

### INGREDIENTS
¼ cup butter
1 small onion
2–3 cloves garlic
about 3 Tbsp. flour
2–2½ cups milk
salt, pepper, and nutmeg to taste
½ cup shredded mozzarella
4–6 Tbsp. grated Parmesan cheese

**TO TIME** this out just right, I started by figuring out which of the three steps would take the longest. I figured it would be the pasta, because the water would take some time to boil, then the chicken, and finally the sauce. They don't all really have to come out at the same time, but you want it to be pretty close so no one element has too much time to cool.

I started by lighting up a full chimney of coals. Once I got some white on them, I set them under the 10-inch Dutch oven, about half to ¾ full of water. I set the lid on the Dutch oven because I can never get enough heat to boil water uncovered. Also, all throughout the steps, I kept adding more coals to the chimney to keep plenty of fresh coals.

While that was starting up, I added some more coals to the chimney and began preparing the chicken. I took out the thawed chicken breasts and laid them out on paper towels to pat them dry (both sides). Then I sprinkled them pretty liberally with the spice mix and let them sit for a while to absorb the flavors.

Meanwhile, I spritzed the inside of a 12-inch Dutch oven with a bit of oil spray and put the Dutch on the coals. After it had been on for 5–10 minutes, I drizzled in the olive oil and let that heat to a simmer. The Dutch oven was quite hot by this time. I put the chicken breasts in the Dutch oven, and they immediately started sizzling. I let them sit, cooking uncovered, for several minutes.

It was at about this point that I could see that the water in the 10-inch oven was boiling, so I added the pasta and set the lid back on.

I turned the chicken breasts over and let them sear on the other side.

At this point, I also put the 8-inch Dutch oven on some coals and put in the butter to melt. While that was going, I quickly diced the onion and minced the garlic and tossed them into the melted butter to sauté.

During this time, I kept checking the pasta, waiting for it to get to the al dente stage. I also lifted the chicken Dutch oven off the coals and adjusted the numbers of the coals so there were 13–15 on the lid and 12–14 below. This changes it from a frying configuration to more of a baking/roasting configuration. I let the chicken finish cooking through.

I added the flour a tablespoon at a time to the butter and onions and stirred with a spatula to make the roux. I was looking for it to be thick but still a bit runny. I let that cook for a bit too. I still wanted it to be blond, not red or brown, so I didn't cook it too long. I added the milk and the spices and put the lid on.

When the pasta was al dente, I pulled it off the coals and drained the pasta with a colander. I poured the pasta back into the Dutch oven to keep it warm. At this point, the chicken was cooked all the way through. While I was waiting for the milk to boil, I sliced the chicken with long diagonal cuts.

Once the milk was boiling, I added the cheeses and kept stirring while they melted. I used brick Parmesan because I like the stronger flavor.

Then, I brought it all together. Pasta, a couple of spoonfuls of sauce on top, and a few slices of chicken on top of that. It was delicious! The harsh picante and the savory chicken helped to counterbalance the undertone of the pasta, and the sharpness of the cheese in the sauce gave it the perfect touch.

# Northeastern

## PHILLY STEAK SANDWICHES

Last spring while I was at a family party, one of my sisters-in-law made some steak sandwiches. She bought the buns and made the meat in her slow cooker. Well, my mind instantly went to the Dutch oven. I started thinking of how I could make the same thing. But just doing the meat and the veggies would be too easy, of course. I needed to challenge myself. So I decided that I would make the buns too. I found a recipe for hoagie rolls and went shopping for some meat and veggies. I was ready to give it a try!

## THE BUNS

### TOOLS

2 (12-inch) shallow Dutch ovens
10 coals below
20 coals above

### INGREDIENTS

3 cups water (½ cup to start, 2½ cups later)
5 tsp. yeast
2 Tbsp. sugar (1 Tbsp. to start, 1 later)
¼ cup vegetable oil
1 Tbsp. salt
about 8 cups flour (4 at first, add rest as you knead)
spray oil

## THE MEAT

### TOOLS

10-inch Dutch oven
15–18 coals below

### INGREDIENTS

1–1½ lbs. finely sliced steak beef (I used "stir-fry" beef, but I'm told you can get any cut of beef sliced Philly-style)
1–2 Tbsp. oil
liberal shakes of steak seasoning mix

2 medium onions
1 green bell pepper
1 red bell pepper
1 jalapeño
2–3 Tbsp. fresh chopped chives
1 cup fresh sliced mushrooms
liberal shakes of salt
1–2 Tbsp. flour
a little water

**I STARTED** by mixing ½ cup warm water with the yeast and 1 tablespoon sugar. I left it to foam up, and it did, pretty readily (about 5 minutes).

Then, in a mixing bowl, I put the rest of the water, the rest of the sugar, the oil, and the salt. To that, I added the yeast mixture.

I dumped in the first four cups of flour and started mixing. It was quite sticky. I started adding the rest of the flour 1 cup at a time, stirring as I did. I used pretty much the full 8 cups. Afterward, I kneaded it until it all stuck together in a ball. Then I pulled it out of the bowl, set it onto the floured table, and started kneading in earnest. I kneaded for a while, sprinkling on a little bit of flour as needed to keep it from sticking. I did the windowpane test by stretching a dough ball until it either became translucent or it tore. I scraped out the bowl and sprayed it with oil and put in the dough ball. I finished that off by spraying the top of the dough with oil and covering it all with a plastic bag.

After about 45 minutes, it had risen pretty well, so I started the coals on fire. I was a bit nervous about that because it was sprinkling rain when I started them, but that was the last of the rain that day! You always gotta watch the weather.

Back to the dough. I punched it down and cut it into 10–12 equal pieces. I rolled them in my hands and cut diagonal slices across the top. That allows the steam to escape the bread. I put them into the 12-inch Dutch ovens as best I could; I tried to make at least an empty inch between each long dough ball. I took the ovens outside and let them sit, "proofing" the bread for another 15–20 minutes while the coals got hot.

Finally, I put them on the coals. It took a good 30 coals for each oven. I also added more to that so I'd have enough hot coals for the meat.

I put the 10-inch Dutch oven on a bed of coals and packed them in underneath as best I could. Then I dumped in the meat pieces with the oil in the bottom. I cooked the meat, browning it, with a bit of stirring until it was pretty much cooked through. I also added liberal shakes of steak seasoning here.

While the meat was cooking, in between stirrings, I jumped inside and sliced up the veggie ingredients. I sliced the jalapeños pretty thin and halved them. I don't like to get a big bite of chili surprise, but I do like the edge it gives the rest of the food. I put all the veggies in with the meat and stirred it all up. I covered it and stirred it occasionally.

Meanwhile, the bread was cooking. The coal count should have brought it up to 400 degrees. I baked it for about 30 minutes. I checked the internal temperature, and once it got to 200 degrees, I pulled them off the coals, out of the Dutch ovens, and onto cooling racks.

By this time, the veggies were cooked pretty nicely. There was some water in the Dutch oven from the veggies and the meat, so I sprinkled on a little flour to thicken it up. My wife suggested a bit more "sauce" as we were eating, so I included the suggestion of a little water in the

Dutch oven as it's cooking. But I'm not convinced it needed it.

Finally, it was all ready to serve! We sliced open the buns and filled them up with steak and veggies. We added a little mayo and mustard, and topped it with some swiss cheese. I was amazed. I think it was one of the best hot sandwiches I have ever tasted. And it was filling too. I couldn't eat another bite to save my life. Hours later, I was still full, just starting to feel like I could have a little som'pm som'pm for dessert.

## SEAFOOD CHOWDER

### (WITHOUT A NET)

This recipe marked a kind of exciting moment for me in my culinary progress—one of the first times I cooked completely without a recipe to guide me. It was very exciting to fly without a net, so to speak, and to have it turn out so well.

To kind of capture that adventurous spirit, I've written this more as a prosaic story rather than a recipe with ingredients and instructions. If you want to cook this, I'd say to read it through first and get an idea of what kinds of things to gather and add in. Then, just follow the process!

This seafood chowder would have been clam chowder, but we were out of those little cans of clams, and instead we had the little cans of crab and shrimp (about the size of tuna cans, you know).

**THE FIRST** thing I did, after lighting up some coals, was get out one of my smaller Dutch ovens and put it on top of about 15 coals or so, so it was getting good and hot. Into it, I put a half of a one-pound package of bacon, cut and separated into little squares. That started cooking.

Once that was going, I got out my 12-inch Dutch oven, which was the one that I was going to do the actual chowder in, and got it on some coals, probably around 20. I had diced up some onions and minced up some garlic (a couple of cloves), and I got that browning in that 12-inch Dutch oven. At this point, there were no lids on and, obviously, no coals on top.

While that was cooking, I was in the kitchen, quartering and slicing the potatoes and slicing some celery. I did about four potatoes and three or four stalks of celery.

Pretty soon, the bacon was nice and crisp and the onions were starting to brown. It was a pretty cheap brand of bacon, so there was lots of grease left in the smaller Dutch oven. I pulled the bacon out and put it in with the onions and left the drippings. To that, I added some flour. You don't want to add it too quickly, because you could easily add too much. I added until it was a little runnier than cookie dough. I just let it cook.

I wanted to see what happened as you cook a roux longer and longer, so I let it go for a while. It gradually got more and more brown. Finally, I saw that it was getting nice and tanned, so I pulled that Dutch oven off the coals.

In the meantime, the onions, garlic, and bacon were still browning nicely in the other Dutch oven. I added a pint carton of cream and about half that much of milk, maybe less. To help it to boil, I put the lid on.

Once it was boiling, I added the potatoes, the celery, and three little cans of seafood, with the liquid. I figured the seafood stock in the cans would enhance the flavor. Once it was boiling again, I added some of the roux, about a tablespoon at a time, stirring vigorously to break it up in the soup. I watched carefully after each tablespoonful of roux for a minute to check the thickness before adding more. If it goes too thick, I guess you can always just add more milk, but I don't want to catch myself adding and adding to catch up with myself over and over again.

Pretty soon, it was nice and thick but still more of a soup than a sauce. You can make it how you like it.

At that point, I added some parsley, salt, and pepper (to taste on all three) and also some lemon juice. Then I pulled some of the coals out from under, so it would go from boil to simmer, and put the lid back on.

I would check it about every 15 minutes, just to taste the potatoes. It didn't take long, maybe 45 minutes, for the chowder to be done.

I was quite proud of it. It helped me to learn how to make more sauces, like the Alfredo sauce (page 44).

# EUROPE

**MUCH OF** our American cuisine has roots in Europe, mainly because so many of us can trace our ancestries back to that continent. American cuisine came across with the colonizers, stayed, and continued to develop. For me, it's fun to learn the dishes of my distant ancestors, who came from the British Isles, Scandinavia, and Germany. But I also like to explore cuisines from other nations around them. Maybe those countries will adopt me . . .

## Greek

### BAKLAVA

I love baklava.

Let me say that again and make it more clear:

I LOVE BAKLAVA.

Truly, it is the dessert of the gods.

And making it is a lot of fun. It's simple yet complex. It's pleasant yet elegant. Few ingredients combine for amazing flavor. It's labor-intensive, but every delicate bite is worth the effort. It's . . . yeah . . . you get the point. Plus, I think that baklava's calories don't count, right?

Michelle, my wife's cousin, taught me how to make it. She has lived in the

Middle East and has gotten quite good at Mediterranean food. She told me that when I had asked her to help me make baklava she had been surprised and wondered if it could be done in a Dutch oven. I love to try and cook things in Dutch ovens that aren't supposed to be!

This one will be a little bit difficult to write up, because Michelle is much more of a free spirit in the kitchen. Be warned that many of the amounts that I've listed here are approximations and guesses. I remember the ingredients we used, but the measurements aren't so critical. I think that much of the success of baklava is in the process, not so much in the exact amounts.

**TOOLS**

12-inch shallow Dutch oven
12–14 coals below
24–28 coals above

**INGREDIENTS**

2 cups walnuts, chopped
¼ cup brown sugar
liberal shakes of cinnamon

2 sticks butter
about 1 lb. phyllo dough

## THE SYRUP

**TOOLS**

8-inch Dutch oven
10–12 coals underneath

**INGREDIENTS**

½ cup honey
¼ cup sugar
water to make a medium-thick syrup

**WE STARTED** by mixing the first set of ingredients. It does work better if the brown sugar is fresh; otherwise, you'll have hard chunks to break up. Not fun.

Then it was time to make the layers. We simply melted the butter in the microwave. It would be easy enough to simply put the 8-inch Dutch oven on a few coals and melt it that way. In fact, you could keep a few coals on it during the layering process to keep it from cooling and solidifying. You don't want to boil it.

Then, we unrolled the phyllo dough (store-bought) from the package. It was a wide rectangular stack, which we cut in half (to a little bigger than a normal sheet of paper). The two halves were stacked on top of each other and then put on top of and underneath sheets of wax paper. That was all topped with a slightly damp towel, to keep the phyllo dough moist.

With a pastry brush, we spread a little butter in the bottom of the Dutch oven and then spread one of the sheets of phyllo dough. With the brush, we brushed butter in the corners of the "paper" and gently over the dough's surface. The next one we put in the same way, but at a 90-degree angle. We brushed butter onto that one as well. We went on stacking—layering phyllo, butter, phyllo, butter—each sheet at a 90-degree angle, crossways from the one below it. I wondered if it would work to do it at a 60-degree angle instead. I doubt it would have made much difference.

After about a third of the total layers of phyllo dough, we spread an even layer (not too thick) of the nut and sugar mixture, enough to cover the dough. You shouldn't be able to see through the nuts to the dough, but no deeper than that. If you don't already have coals burning, you should go out and light them at this point. We already had coals lit and cooking some dolmades (see next recipe).

Then, we got back to the layering, for another third of the dough. We followed that with another spread of nuts and sugar. At this point, your coals should be nice and hot. We put a whole bunch on the Dutch oven lid and let it preheat. Finally, we layered the rest of the dough.

The next step was to get a knife and cut the slices. This is where we made the diamond pattern, characteristic of baklava. (I don't know if this is anything other than tradition. It could be rooted in some esoteric cooking reasoning. I don't know why it's done. You do need to cut it, and it needs to be cut at this stage because it will be too crisp and crackly to cut later, and the syrup needs to be able to run down into the baklava. However, I don't know why it should be done in diamonds.)

Once it's cut, put it on the coals and let it start baking.

While that was cooking, we made the syrup. Simply combine the syrup set of ingredients and simmer until it's the right consistency. Not as thick as the honey, but not as runny as the water. Somewhere in between.

We cooked the baklava for about 30–40 minutes. When the top layer was a nice golden brown, it was time to take it off.

With the baklava baked and brown and the syrup ready, we simply poured the syrup over the baklava. It ran into the cracks between the baklava pieces that were cut and soaked into the phyllo dough layers. That gave it that sticky, gooey sweetness that we all love so much about baklava.

Then, we let it cool a little and served it up! Ours didn't last long, so I have no idea how long it'll keep!

## DOLMADES

When I first heard of dolmades (or "dolmas," or just "rolled grape leaves"), I was kinda grossed out. They didn't sound good. But once I had tried them, I was hooked. I love these things! And when I started doing Dutch ovens, I knew that at some point I was going to try to make them.

My wife's cousin Michelle came over and showed me how to do it at the same time that we made the Baklava (page 51).

As I was preparing to write the recipe here, I did a little research and confirmed some things I already knew. Like, that there are *soooo* many variations of this dish that you really can't do it wrong. Even from family to family, the flavor and the recipes change so much. It all remains similar, but don't be afraid to make it your own.

### TOOLS

12-inch Dutch oven
20+ coals below for the meat filling
12–15 coals above and below for the final cooking.

### INGREDIENTS

olive oil
1 medium to large onion
3–4 cloves garlic
salt
1–1½ lbs. ground meat (pretty much any kind except pork or sausage)
1–2 Tbsp. baharat or other spices or flavorings, as you choose, like:

- cinnamon
- allspice
- minced fresh parsley
- minced fresh mint leaves
- pine nuts
- lemon zest
- salt
- pepper

1½ cups uncooked rice

grape leaves, blanched

2–3 tomatoes, chopped (optional)
additional optional flavorings:
- 2–3 cloves garlic, sliced
- lemon juice and lemon slices
- ground cloves

3 cups chicken stock or water

**I STARTED** this adventure by putting about 20 coals under a Dutch oven with a little oil in the bottom. I diced up an onion and minced the garlic cloves and, when the oil was hot enough, tossed them in to sauté. If they sizzle and jump right away, you know it's hot enough. I shook on a little salt too.

Once the onions were browned a little, I added in the meat. This time, I used ground turkey. If I can acquire it next time, I'll use lamb, but ordinary ground beef is okay too. As that was browning, I added in the baharat. Baharat is a mix of spices commonly used in Turkish and Middle Eastern cooking. You can buy it at a specialty market, or, using the Internet as a guide, mix your own from the optional spices listed. Really, the seasonings and the flavorings are completely up to you. Again, there are so many regional and familial variations on this dish that you really can't go wrong.

Once this is cooked, I pulled it off the heat and let it cool some. Then I added in the rice as part of the filling. Don't cook the rice. That will come later. With all this, the filling is ready.

I rinsed out the Dutch oven and wiped it down. I spread a little olive oil in the bottom, and we got ready to roll the dolmas. I used pre-blanched grape leaves straight from a bottle that I bought at a Greek market. I don't have any grape vines. Oh well.

One suggestion that Michelle made was to spread a layer of chopped tomatoes over the bottom of the pan, to raise up the dolmas and make them not burn or stick to the pan. That sounded like a great idea, but we didn't have any tomatoes. You try it and tell me how it works. Instead, we covered the bottom of the pan with one layer of flat grape leaves.

So, here's how to roll the dolmas:

1. Separate out a grape leaf, and pinch off any of the stem that's left.
2. Lay it flat, with the vein side up, and unfold it if there are any folds.

3. Spread a finger-width spot of filling (about 2 finger joints long) on the leaf. Put it just above where the stem was.
4. Fold the lower part of the leaf up and over the filling.
5. Fold the sides inward, over the filling.
6. Roll it the rest of the way up.
7. Place it on the leaves or the tomatoes in the bottom of the Dutch oven.
8. Do it again, making a single layer of dolmas.
9. Keep going. You can add on a second layer if you have enough leaves and filling.

After we'd rolled up all of our filling, I added some of the garlic slices and lemon slices on top. Then we poured on the stock. The dolmas tended to float a little, and Michelle said you can put a plate on them to weigh them down.

This went on the coals. I used the coals listed, with the Dutch oven lid on. You don't need to cook it long, just to cook the rice and the leaves. Maybe 10–15 minutes once it's boiling. I would watch for venting steam out of the lid of the Dutch oven and pull them off about 10 minutes or so later.

Now, at this point, we were pretty busy making the soup and the baklava, so I didn't make any of the cucumber yogurt sauce (tzatziki) that I love so much with dolmades. But, I did search for a recipe and made this adaptation:

## TZATZIKI

### INGREDIENTS

1 cucumber
1 cup plain yogurt
2 cloves garlic, finely chopped
¼ tsp. salt
1 tsp. chopped fresh mint leaves
a spritz or two of lemon juice

**FIRST, PEEL** the cucumber and halve or quarter it lengthwise. Use a spoon to scoop out the seeds and then a coarse grater to grate it into bits. You could cube it if you prefer. Add the other ingredients and chill it all for at least 30 minutes to develop the flavor. When you eat the dolmades, you dip them in the tzatziki.

## GREEK MEATBALLS

As I cook each Sunday afternoon, at times I have trouble thinking of things to cook. One week my wife bought me some ground lamb, and I'd been eager to try it. But I actually struggled with trying to figure out what to do with it. I'd looked all over the Internet looking for ideas and finally found something I could adapt.

#### TOOLS

12-inch Dutch oven
15–18 coals below

#### INGREDIENTS

4 slices white bread
2 Tbsp. milk
3 cloves garlic, minced
1 onion, diced and minced
a bundle of fresh mint, chopped, without the stems
salt and ground black pepper to taste
½ lb. ground beef
½ lb. ground lamb
4 eggs

olive oil for frying

½ cup flour for dredging, plus a little more for the pan sauce

about ½ cup water
juice from 1 lemon

### THE RICE

#### TOOLS

8-inch Dutch oven
10 coals below

#### INGREDIENTS

1 cup rice
2 cups turkey broth

**AFTER GETTING** some coals started, I started preparing the ingredients. I tore the bread into pieces and put them in a bowl with the milk to soak. I minced up the garlic and diced up the onions. Finally, I added everything in that first set into a big bowl and stirred it all up. I made sure it was all blended by mushing it together with my fingers. I formed the mess into meatballs, about 1–1½ inches in diameter.

Then I got the Dutch oven on the coals with a little bit of oil in the bottom. I let it heat up, but not too much. I dredged the meatballs in the flour and dropped them into the Dutch oven to start cooking.

Here's where I learned to be a bit cautious. At first, I had quite a bit of heat, but that made them brown too quickly. So, I kept the heat a little more moderate so the meatballs cooked through a little more slowly. I turned them with some cooking tongs, from time to time. I actually had to cook them in a couple of batches, because there wasn't room in one Dutch oven for them. I put a few coals under a second 12-inch Dutch oven (maybe 6–8 coals) and used it, with the lid on, as a warmer for the ones that were done.

Somewhere during the cooking of the second half of these, I put some rice on in my 8-inch Dutch oven. I put about a cup of rice in with about 2 cups of turkey broth. I put that over about 10 coals. When it started steaming out from under the lid, I let it cook for another 10 minutes and then pulled it off and let it sit, covered for ten more.

While all this cooking was happening, I had an intriguing thought to make a pan sauce out of all that delicious, crusty fond that had been building up on the bottom of the Dutch oven. Once all of the meatballs were warming in the other oven, I set to making the pan sauce in the original frying oven. First, I poured in about a half cup of water, and about a lemon's worth of juice. It immediately began sizzling. I took a wooden spoon and started scraping up the bits off the bottom of the Dutch oven. It only took a minute or two before all that crusty stuff was swimming in a bubbling broth.

I put in a bit of flour, shaking it in a little at a time, while stirring and whisking, to thicken it up. Soon it was ready. I put the meatballs from the warming pot back into the sauce, stirred it up, and served it over the rice.

It was delicious! The lamb is savory, of course, but it's a totally different flavor than ground beef. The spices enhanced the savory tones, and the sour of the lemon in the pan sauce was delicious.

## Italian

I really love Italian-based dishes. I say "Italian-based" because I know I can't do authentic Italian like someone's Sicilian grandma. Still, pasta is a staple at our house, especially on the weeknights, when I typically cook

indoors, not in my Dutch ovens. My first Dutch oven dinner ever, back when my wife bought me my first one, was pizza. I love the smell of garlic and herbs in tomatoes. And the cheeses! Don't get me started!

Oops. Too late . . .

## LASAGNA

It's always fun to make lasagna in my Dutch oven. It's fun because I often get a reaction like, "Lasagna? In a Dutch oven? Is that . . . um . . . legal?"

I love it when people react like that!

And this one is pretty easy to do. It's a two-step recipe, but neither step is complex. Brown the sausage and then make the layers and bake. Unlike most indoor lasagna recipes, you don't need to cook the noodles first. In the times before, I mixed the ricotta with the sauce, but this time, I didn't. I like the separate layers; it makes the tastes more distinct.

### TOOLS

10-inch Dutch oven
8 coals below
16 coals above

### INGREDIENTS

3 large links (12-oz.) mild-to-medium Italian sausage
1 medium onion, chopped
2 Tbsp. minced garlic

3 (8-oz.) cans tomato sauce
1 (6-oz.) can tomato paste
a couple of hefty shakes of oregano
a mild shake of basil
salt to taste
pepper
paprika

1 box (12-oz.) uncooked lasagna noodles
16 oz. ricotta cheese
shredded mozzarella

**TO START** with, I fired up a lot of coals. As they got white, I layered about 20 of them flat and close together and put the Dutch oven with the sausage (crumbled) in it. I browned the sausage. I tossed in the onions and the garlic and let them sauté too.

While this was going on, I mixed up the tomato sauce and the spices. When the sausage and onions were done, I added the sauce in and stirred it all up.

Then, I made a stack of layers in the Dutch oven. From the bottom, those layers were:

- a thin layer of the sauce mix
- a layer of dry, uncooked noodles
- a layer of ricotta cheese
- a layer of mozzarella
- a layer of sauce mix
- more noodles
- more ricotta (the last of it)
- more mozzarella
- more sauce
- more noodles
- a little more sauce

Finally, I smothered the whole thing in mozzarella.

I spread the coals into a ring of 8 and set the Dutch oven on it. Then I put 16 burning coals on top. I baked it for about 45 minutes, turning the oven and the lid every 20 minutes or so. The cool thing about it is that the moisture in the sauce and the ricotta will cook the noodles soft so you don't have to precook them. It's really delicious.

## PENNE RUSTICA AND PARMESAN-SEASONED BREADSTICKS

My good friend John (of mormonfoodie.com) is partly responsible for the existence of Mark's Black Pot. He and I have been really good friends for a long time. We also worked together, and our offices were right next to each other. We got together in our downtime at work (mostly at lunch) to talk religion, politics, and food. He's the one that taught me how to make a killer omelet.

When he started his Mormon Foodie blog, it wasn't long before that inspired me to start writing down my recipes and stories.

So, when he started writing a month-long series on pasta, I couldn't help but join in. At that point, I'd already done lasagna and spaghetti. Later, I'd try tortellini and a few others. I even made pasta from scratch.

This particular week, I had found a chain restaurant knock-off recipe for a penne rustica. I love eating at this restaurant, and when we go there, we always get that dish. So I was eager to give this a try. As it turned out, it was some of the most delicious pasta I've ever tasted, and certainly the best I have ever cooked myself. I don't really know that it's a good knockoff of the original, but it was quite good.

## THE PENNE RUSTICA

### TOOLS

10-inch Dutch oven
lots of coals below and above

12-inch deep Dutch oven
11 coals below
20 coals above

### INGREDIENTS

water
1 lb. penne rigate, cooked

1 lb. skinless chicken breasts or tenderloins
1 lb. medium shrimp, peeled and deveined

3 Tbsp. olive oil
2 Tbsp. minced garlic
3 Tbsp. white grape juice
4 oz. prosciutto, chopped

2 cups heavy cream
1 cup grated Parmesan cheese
½ cup milk
½ cup chicken broth
1 Tbsp. cornstarch
1 Tbsp. Dijon mustard
shakes of rosemary, salt, thyme, ground cayenne pepper
shakes of oregano, paprika

1 (16-oz.) bag of grated mozzarella or Asiago cheese (or a blend)

**I STARTED** up some coals right away. As soon as the coals were ready, I put some water on to boil in the 10-inch Dutch oven. As soon as that was boiling, I put in the penne.

In the meantime, I worked on the other parts. It was really quite hectic to prepare, rushing here and there to get all the steps done. Make sure you read through this recipe and plan it out, or you'll get lost.

The next step was to get the chicken and the shrimp ready. This is where I kinda cheated, but the results tasted great. I took the chicken (I used tenderloins) and the shrimp and put them in a big bowl. I shook in some olive oil and salt and pepper and stirred it up. Then I put the shrimp and chicken on skewers and fired up the grill. That's kinda cheating, because in cook-offs you have to do all the cooking in Dutch ovens. But I loved the grilled flavor on the chicken and the shrimp.

Then I got out the 12-inch deep oven and put some coals under it. I put in the olive oil and then the garlic, grape juice, and proscuitto. I stirred it and cooked it a bit.

While that was cooking, I mixed up the sauce ingredients (everything else except the mozzarella and asiago) in a bowl. By this time, the penne was cooked (partly boiled, partly steamed in the Dutch oven), so I added it to the deep Dutch oven and poured in the sauce mix. Then I put in some of the cheese and stirred it all up to get it well mixed. Finally, I covered the top with the rest of the cheeses and put it in the heat with the listed amount of coals. I cooked it for 25–35 minutes, turning the Dutch oven once.

While that was cooking, my wife had suggested I make some breadsticks with seasonings and Parmesan cheese. She showed me a recipe in an old cookbook. I admit I was a bit skeptical. It was a yeast bread recipe, but the rise time was really short and the instructions were really strange. But I decided to give it a shot.

## THE PARMESAN-SEASONED BREADSTICKS

### TOOLS

12-inch Dutch oven
12 coals below, 22 above

### INGREDIENTS

1½ cups warm water
1 Tbsp. yeast
1 Tbsp. honey

1 tsp. salt
about 4 cups flour
¼ cup butter, melted
liberal shakes of Parmesan cheese and other seasonings

**FIRST, I** put the water, yeast, and honey in a bowl and let the yeast activate. Then I added the salt and the flour. Don't add all the flour in at once, because then you can gauge the moistness and the density of the dough. I kneaded it for 10 minutes.

Then I poured the melted butter in the bottom of the 12-inch oven and spread the dough out over it. I cut the dough into strips and then sprinkled on the Parmesan and the seasonings (I used this really great salad seasoning combo). At that point, I set it aside for about 20–30 minutes to rise. That's it. No long rising or proofing.

Finally, once it had risen some, I put it on the coals. In about 20–30 minutes, they were done. And they were delicious!

And the penne was incredible. It was really filling—and wow, what a dinner!

## HANDMADE HERB FETTUCCINI WITH CREAMY CHICKEN SAUCE

The more and more I do Dutch oven cookery, the more I've come to realize that becoming skilled at Dutch oven cookery is really more about becoming a real chef that happens to use a Dutch oven as their cooking system of choice. Now, in saying that, I am, by no means, claiming to be a chef. I'm learning to cook, and along the way, some folks tell me that they like what I cook. Sometimes. Well, they usually do, because the times that I flop, I usually don't force other people to eat it.

That's another story for another day.

What I *am* saying, however, is that as I learn "how to cook in a Dutch oven," I'm seeing more and more that what I'm really learning is more "how to cook"—in a Dutch oven. Teaching myself is one thing, and following recipes is one thing, but knowing what I'm really doing is another altogether!

What I'm leading up to is that on the night I did this recipe, I took a major step forward in learning "how to cook." I made my own pasta from scratch.

It's all John's fault. See, he got me started when, over at mormonfoodie.com, he blogged for a whole month about pasta and even made some of his own. That inspired me. I knew we had one of those cool roller things, so this was going to be easy. But then I couldn't find it.

That's okay, though, because I had remembered seeing in one of my books a series of instructional photos on how to roll and stretch out pasta. I dug for it, looked it up, and I couldn't make any sense out of it. I read it and reread it and studied the pictures. I could tell this was gonna be a "you had to be there" kinda thing.

Then, I wondered if there might be someone somewhere that had made a video online of it. And there was! I found one of this nice old Italian lady mixing and rolling out the pasta. And the rolling she's doing looks very much like the pictures in the book I had! I studied the videos and figured out what she was doing. Then, I tried it myself! It was *so* much fun. I made the noodles and cooked them up.

Since then, as I've practiced this technique more and more, I've made a video of the process on my own. I've put it up on my YouTube channel, which can be found at www.youtube.com/mrkhmusic. Click on "Uploads." Or the direct URL to the video itself is www.youtube.com/watch?v=rQMWEUI8AxU.

### TOOLS

2 (12-inch) shallow Dutch ovens
20+ coals under each one

### INGREDIENTS

**The Handmade Pasta Fresca**

2 cups flour (you'll use more for rolling later)
½ tsp. salt
1 Tbsp. parsley
1 Tbsp. oregano
1 Tbsp. garlic powder
3 eggs
¼ cup water

**The Creamy Chicken Sauce**

1 onion, sliced
1–2 Tbsp. minced garlic
4 oz. sliced fresh mushrooms
olive oil
water
1–2 lbs. chicken, sliced or cubed (I used frozen breasts, slightly thawed)
3 Tbsp. butter
¼ cup flour

2 cups milk
¼ cup balsamic vinegar
2–3 Tbsp. sun-dried tomatoes in oil
salt
pepper
parsley

**THE PASTA** is one situation where I like using garlic powder instead of minced garlic. I've tried making pasta with the mince, and the chunks get in the way when the pasta is thin. I don't use semolina flour. I've tried it, and I actually prefer all-purpose. I've heard of some people mixing it half and half, but I haven't done that yet.

Anyway. The first thing to do was to mix up all the pasta ingredients. In the video, the lady makes a volcano of flour and dry ingredients, puts the eggs in the middle, and then mixes it up with a fork. I tried that and it got all over. Still, I managed to mix it all up and not get it on the floor.

Once that was all mixed, I kneaded it for 8–10 minutes, just like I knead bread, shaking bits of flour on the table as I went. Then I set it on the table top to rest for a while.

Then, I went to get my stick! About a week before, I had bought a yard-long, 1½-inch diameter dowel. After watching the videos, I could tell that a simple rolling pin wasn't going to cut it. It would simply not be long enough, and that proved to be true, even though I didn't make as much as the lady in the videos. Still, I could tell that three feet was gonna be too much for my little kitchen counter, so I cut about a foot off of one end. I sanded it very smooth and then treated it with olive oil.

I started just like in the video. I rolled it out to a disc maybe a little under a foot in diameter just like I would do with a normal rolling pin. Then I rubbed on a light layer of flour, flipped the far edge up and over and rolled it up, and started the rolling and stretching process.

Here's how it works: I applied a bit of rolling pressure as I moved the stick toward me. Then I released the pressure and slid the stick (without rolling it) away from me. Then I rolled it toward me again. Actually, I was doing a bit of back-and-forth rocking motion as I rolled the stick toward me. While I was doing this, I was moving my hands "outward" to help stretch the dough side to side.

Then I unrolled it, turned it a little, rolled it up again, and worked it the same way. Just like in the video. Each time I unrolled it, I watched to see if it was sticking at all. If so, I smoothed on some flour. Gradually, it got thinner and thinner, and bigger and bigger. I gotta tell you too how goooooood it smelled while I was rolling it out. Those herbs and the garlic had me in heaven.

Finally, as the video instructs, I folded it up and sliced it. Really, I probably sliced it too thick to call it true fettuccini. After slicing it, I lightly tossed it with my fingers to separate it and left it on the tabletop to dry a little. I didn't let it dry out, though. I could have, but I didn't. Then it wouldn't have been pasta fresca, but rather pasta secca (dry pasta rather than fresh pasta).

Then on to the sauce:

I started with the onion, the garlic, and the mushrooms, sautéing them in one of the Dutch ovens in a bit of olive oil. The other one had water on, so it could get boiling. I keep it covered, because it boils faster that way.

Once the onions and the mushrooms were browning, I added the chicken. I like to keep the lid on when I cook frozen chicken this way because it tends to steam the chicken and keep it moist.

Once the chicken was cooked through, I added the butter and the flour. The butter melted, along with the oil, and made a bit of a roux. I added all the other ingredients, and let it simmer, stirring it often. This was all done with the lid off.

Somewhere in all that, I checked and saw the water boiling. A pasta book I had been reading during this whole adventure said to put the pasta in gradually so it doesn't stop the boil. I did this and put the lid back on to help it come back to a full boil. I only cooked it for a few minutes once it started boiling again. I tested it for al dente, and it was there! I drained the pasta in a colander in the sink and served it up with the sauce and some Parmesan cheese. It was fantastic!

I also tasted several strands of the pasta by itself and enjoyed the herbs and the flavor. It was yummy just as it was! The sauce was great with it too.

I learned an important lesson: how to make pasta from scratch. I enjoyed it. It was work, but it didn't take very long. I think next time, I'll make more and dry some out. The results were certainly delicious!

# HANDMADE TORTELLINI WITH ALFREDO SAUCE

My first experience making pasta encouraged me, emboldened me, and I decided to try it again, with a twist. My favorite pasta of all is tortellini. I love it with an Alfredo sauce and a link or two of italian sausage. I wanted to make that and make the tortellini myself. The first time I tried, I bungled the Alfredo sauce, and it was horrible. The second time, however, was magical. This was the result.

I tried making this a long time ago, but I didn't write about it because the sauce was absolutely horrible. It "broke." That means that the cheese ended up in a coagulated mass, and the milk was runny. Yuck. It was one of my worst tanks.

So I thought I'd try it again, now that I've learned how to do sauces better.

I'll have to warn you: the way I did this was with a complex process. It's not for beginners. I started in the morning, and it all ended at about 5:00 p.m. Of course, there was a lot of downtime in the middle. Still, there are a lot of steps.

## THE FILLING

### TOOLS

8-inch Dutch oven
12–15 coals below

### INGREDIENTS

1–2 cups chopped fresh spinach
4 green onions, chopped
handful of chopped fresh parsley
½ cup water
1 small tub ricotta cheese
salt
juice of 1 lemon

**I STARTED** early in the day by putting some coals under my 8-inch Dutch oven, and I put the spinach, onions, parsley, and water inside. I set the lid on and let it boil down until the spinach greens were soft.

Once that was boiled down and all the greens were soft, I took the vegetables out and put them in a colander to drain and cool. Once they were cool, I put them in a bowl and added the ricotta, salt, and lemon juice and stirred it all up. I put this in the fridge, covered by plastic wrap.

## THE TORTELLINI

### INGREDIENTS

2 cups flour
6 eggs
handful of chopped parsley
2 Tbsp. minced garlic
pinch of salt

**I MADE** the tortellini using the method for the pasta fresca on pages 64–66. This recipe is just a bit different than the one I'd used before. It's not "specially formulated for tortellini"; it's just different. You can use either one.

Once I had it all rolled out, I used a small kids' cup (with a diameter of about 2 inches) to cut the discs for the tortellinis. This made them pretty big, but that's okay. They were easier to work with that way.

One thing I'd recommend: Once you've used the cup to cut the discs, gather up the extra pasta and ball it up. Put the discs aside and roll out the extra. Cut more discs and carry on that way until all the dough is used up or you have enough discs. Plan on about 10 tortellinis per serving.

Then I held a disc in my fingers and put about ½ teaspoon of filling into it. I wet the edge of one side with my finger dipped in water and folded it in half. I closed it up, pinching as I went. I had seen a TV show about making potstickers, and it said to press the edges together, starting where the filling is, so there's no air pockets.

Once it's all sealed in a half-circle pouch, I bent each corner inward and made the little "hat" that's tortellini. Once I got going, it went pretty fast. I just set them aside and let them dry a little bit.

## THE SAUCE

### TOOLS

8-inch Dutch oven
10–12 coals below

### INGREDIENTS

1 stick butter
flour

½ medium onion, chopped
¼ cup chopped mushrooms

2 green onions, chopped
1 Tbsp. oil

1 cup heavy cream
1 cup milk
2–3 Tbsp. roux
big pinch of grated romano cheese, to taste
big pinch of grated mozzarella cheese, to taste
big shake of grated Parmesan cheese, to taste
salt
pepper

**BEGIN WITH** the roux: Put an 8-inch Dutch oven onto 10–12 coals and melt a stick of butter in it. Begin adding spoonfuls of flour until it's almost the consistency of cookie dough. Cook it, stirring, until it's just a little more tan than it started. Then take it off the coals. After you're done with the dish, you can put what's left over in a baggie in the fridge.

I started by sautéeing the second set of ingredients until they were quite browned. This actually took quite a long time. Then I pulled them out of the oven and poured in the cream and the milk. I put the lid on and let it start boiling.

Then, I started adding in the roux. I added it gradually, stirring with a whisk, until it was thick enough. I'm estimating the amount in the ingredients above.

Once it was thick, I added the onions and the mushrooms back in, and then I added in the remaining ingredients. I kept whisking and stirring, to keep it going. It was great, and it didn't "break" like last time.

**TOOLS**
12-inch Dutch oven
18–20 coals below
10-inch Dutch oven
15–18 coals below

**INGREDIENTS**
links of mild Italian sausage
water

mizithra cheese (optional)

In the meantime, I had another 12-inch Dutch oven with 18–20 coals underneath cooking some links of mild Italian sausage.

I also had my 10-inch Dutch oven, with 15–18 coals under it. That one was boiling water for the tortellini. Once it was boiling, I put in the tortellini and let it come back to a boil. Once it was back to boiling, it cooked quickly, in about 10 minutes.

After making all these elements, it was fun to finally plate it up and serve it. I dished up some tortellinis and poured on some sauce. Then I sliced up a sausage link and put it on the side. Finally, I scraped some mizithra cheese on top. Yum!

## BRENDON'S BAKED ZITI

One spring day, as we were preparing for a Dutch oven gathering, my son Brendon and I began searching for dishes to cook. He and I had been watching *America's Test Kitchen*, and they had a recipe for a baked ziti pasta dish that you made in one skillet.

Well, then, we could do it in a Dutch oven, right? That was Brendon's choice. So, we figured out how to turn it into a Dutch oven recipe of the highest caliber!

### TOOLS

12-inch Dutch oven
15–20 coals below, then
8–10 coals below, and 18–22 coals above

### INGREDIENTS

6 cloves garlic, chopped
1 medium onion, diced
1 tsp. oil
½ tsp. crushed red pepper (we actually went more toward 1 tsp.)
1 lb. ground meat (we used turkey)

1 (28-oz.) can crushed tomatoes
3 cups water
½ tsp. salt
1 lb. ziti pasta
juice of 1 lemon

1 pint carton cream
½ cup Parmesan cheese
liberal doses of basil, oregano, and parsley
liberal dose of black pepper

1 (16–oz.) package shredded mozzarella
feta, crumbled, for serving

**FIRST OF** all, Brendon got some coals going and then chopped up the garlic and the onion. While that was happening, the oil was getting hot in the Dutch oven. When he dropped in the onions and garlic, we could hear the sizzle and smell the aroma! The red pepper went in too. These all got sautéed. When done, we added the meat to brown.

Once the meat had browned, Brendon opened up the can of tomatoes and poured them in. He added the other ingredients in the second set. (It looks like it will be really runny with all that water, but that and the tomato juice cook the pasta.)

Then he closed the lid. Still using bottom heat, he cooked the pasta for about 20 minutes, until it was al dente. It was yummy to taste test too. Cooking the pasta in the sauce does two things: One, it infuses the pasta with the tomato and onion/garlic flavors, and two, the starch from the pasta thickens the sauce just a little. It's got this symbiotic thing goin' on.

Once the pasta was cooked, we pulled it off the coals. Brendon added the ingredients of the third set, stirred it, and then smothered it in mozzarella. At that point, we put it back on a ring of coals. It wasn't that cold out, so we kept the bottom coals pretty few. Remember that the ingredients are already cooked. We want the cream to come up to temperature and the herbs to spread the flavor, but mostly we want the mozzarella to melt and brown. That's why we went so heavy on top coals.

That baked for another 20 minutes or so, just to get a good bronze goin' on the cheese. Then he pulled it off, let it cool a bit, and served it with crumbled feta. Yum, yum, yum.

And I've gotta say, I'm proud of the guy for trying such a challenging Dutch oven recipe and pulling it off so well.

## MARK'S OWN CALZONE

One day I was at the grocery store, and I saw some premade, bake-them-yourself calzones. They looked really appetizing, even in their uncooked state.

This recipe ended up being a pretty involved two-day affair, because I decided I wanted to try an overnight rise on the crust dough.

## THE CRUST

### INGREDIENTS

1 Tbsp. yeast
1½ cups warm water
1 Tbsp. sugar
¼ tsp. salt
3 Tbsp. oil
4 cups bread flour

## THE FILLING/SAUCE

### TOOLS

10-inch Dutch oven
15–18 coals below

### INGREDIENTS

½ lb. mild Italian sausage
¼ lb. bacon, cut into short strips
1 link of pepperoni, quartered and chopped
1 Tbsp. flour

½ medium onion, diced
2–3 cloves garlic, minced
2 stalks celery, chopped
1 green pepper, chopped
½ jalapeño, seeded, cored, and chopped

6–7 Roma tomatoes, diced
½ cup water

## THE CALZONES

### TOOLS

12-inch Dutch oven
10–12 coals below
16–18 coals above

### INGREDIENTS

2 cups shredded mozzarella
1 egg, beaten

Italian parsley, chopped
Parmesan and/or mizithra cheese, grated

**LIKE I** said, it all started the night before. I had read a lot about how the longer overnight rises are better for pizza, and I thought I'd try it that way. Spoiler alert: I'm definitely sold on that, now.

I proofed the yeast in water that was hot, but not scalding, to the touch. I say it's "shower" hot. That's right around 110–115 degrees, and it's great for waking up yeast. While that's getting foamy and frothy, I added the other crust ingredients to a bowl. The last bit was to add the yeast/water mix.

I stirred it all up and found that it was just the right hydration, this time. I started kneading it on the countertop, and I found I didn't need to add any more flour in the process. I say, "this time" because different flours and different humidities can mean that the flour will absorb more or less water. You just never know.

I set the dough in a greased bowl, covered with plastic wrap, in the fridge. I knew I wasn't going to use it until the next day, and I wanted it to have a long, slow, flavor-developing rise overnight in the fridge.

The next day, I pulled the bread dough out of the fridge and set it aside in the kitchen, to come up to room temperature. I also lit up some coals and put the lightly oiled 10-inch Dutch oven on them to season and heat up. Once it was smoking a little bit, I put in the sausage, the bacon, and the pepperoni pieces. I used link pepperoni and cut it into small chunks, but you could use sliced pepperoni. I'd still probably cut the slices in half or into wedges. The sausage cooked, the bacon crisped, and the pepperoni browned.

Once the meat was all done, I took it out but left the drippings. I sprinkled in the flour and stirred while it cooked into a roux. When it was just a little darker, I pulled it out as best I could. Then, I tossed in the first set of veggies to sweat and sauté. Keep the oven hot all along the way, with fresh coals if you need to.

Finally, I added the tomatoes and the water, and then I brought the meat and the roux back in as well. I let it boil, at first, and then simmer, covered. I gave the tomatoes time to dissolve as much as possible—maybe as much as an hour. It should be nice and "sauce" thick. If it's still too runny at that point, let it cook a bit longer with the lid off.

Taste it all along the way. I'll bet that with all of the sausages and bacon, it won't need much salt, if any, and probably not many other seasonings. Some lemon juice might have been great, in retrospect.

Once the sauce was done simmering, I poured it out of the Dutch oven and into a bowl right away so the tomatoes wouldn't eat away at the patina.

I dumped the bread dough out onto my floured countertop and cut it into quarters. Then I stretched each one out into a circle on the countertop. Each circle should be stretched out wide and thin. I put a generous amount of sauce over one half of each dough circle. I piled it on but left at least a half inch or so to the edge of the dough. I put a generous amount of shredded mozzarella on top of the mound of filling. I brushed some freshly beaten egg onto that edge of the dough, as a sealer. I folded the dough over and began pinching and curling the dough halves together. Finally, I gently lifted the finished calzone into the oiled 12-inch Dutch oven.

I did that for the other three calzones. There should be a good amount of sauce left over. Then, I brushed all the calzones with the beaten egg, giving a good coating. I let that Dutch oven sit, to let the dough continue rising a bit.

In the meantime, I'd been starting up some additional coals, and I put those on the 12-inch lid to heat it up. After the lid was really good and hot, and the dough had proofed just a little bit, I set a ring of coals below the Dutch oven and set the lid with the coals on top.

I watched and maintained the heat with fresh coals, as needed. I took the bread temperature by sticking the thermometer down in between the calzones, where the crusts grew together. Taking the temperature of the filling was kinda pointless since it was all completely cooked already. I let the bread get to a bit over 200 degrees, because I wasn't sure how it would react to the filling. That turned out to be a good thing. It was done perfectly.

Serving was easy. I cut the calzones apart from each other, and I served each with more sauce drizzled over the top and with a garnish of chopped parsley and grated cheese.

It was big and filling, and it had an incredible taste!

## CHICAGO-STYLE PIZZA

On a recent trip back to visit my parents in Indiana, we stopped over for a night with our friend in Chicago, and she treated us to a Chicago-style pizza dinner. It's bigger and heftier than most pizzas, with a sauced-up crust on top as well as on the bottom. Oh, it was so good and so filling. I loved it, and I knew instantly that I had to try doing it in the Dutch oven. It took me a while to get around to it, but I did!

I did some recipe research and found some good ones. There was a lot of variation. I finally settled on a crust recipe and some ideas for the sauce and fillings. I doubled the crust recipe and made two different pies, each with unique fillings. I liked both of the ones I did.

I have to interject a disclaimer here. I know that this is technically the chapter on Italian food. I also know that Chicago-style pizza is NOT authentic Italian food. It's a good example of how Americans have taken traditional cuisines and warped and twisted them beyond recognition. But I'm still going to include it. So nyah, nyah, nyah . . .

That day was drizzly and rainy, so I had to rig a little shelter for my ovens. I was also concerned with the cooking time because the pizza was so much thicker than pizzas I'd cooked before. Between all of that, I ended up cooking it too long. The bottom crust was a little singed, and the top was a bit overly brown as well. It wasn't charred black, but it was overdone. When I do it again, I'll cook it less, and that will be reflected in the instructions below so, hopefully, you won't make my mistake.

### TOOLS

2 (12-inch) Dutch ovens
10–12 coals below each, plus more for earlier steps
18–22 coals above each

## INGREDIENTS

**The Crust**
3 tsp. sugar
2 Tbsp. active dry yeast
1¼ cups warm water
3–4 cups bread flour, divided
3 tsp. salt
½ Tbsp. vital wheat gluten or 3 Tbsp. dough enhancer (optional)
4 Tbsp. olive oil

**The Fillings**
4 oz. shredded mozzarella
(The remaining fillings are optional, but the more the merrier)
½ lb. mild or medium Italian sausage
cubed ham
pepperoni slices
onions, diced
green peppers, diced
Roma tomatoes, diced
baby spinach leaves, julienned
black olives, chopped
fresh mushrooms
anything else you like

garlic powder
salt
olive oil

**The Sauce**
1 (6-oz.) can tomato paste
1 (8-oz.) can tomato sauce
2 fresh Roma tomatoes, diced
3–4 cloves garlic, minced
liberal shakes of:

- oregano
- basil
- rosemary
- salt
- pepper

4 oz. shredded mozzarella

**THIS ADVENTURE** began when I made the bread dough. Like the calzones before (previous recipe), I would actually encourage you to do the dough the night before and let it rise in the fridge. On this particular day, I couldn't make that work.

I did the crust process essentially like every other bread dough I've done. I mixed the sugar, the yeast, and the water. I did that a little more carefully this time, however, because I wanted to keep it at 110–115 degrees. So I poured in the warm water a bit at a time and monitored the temperature as the sugar dissolved, adding hotter water to keep it "in the zone." It rewarded me by foaming up quite nicely.

I sifted the dry ingredients (flour, salt, and gluten) together, starting with just 3 cups of flour. I would add the rest of the flour during kneading. The bread flour I had was getting a bit old, so I added the vital gluten powder. It helped it in the kneading.

Then, I mixed in the wet ingredients (the water/yeast mix and the olive oil) and kneaded it on the table top, adding flour onto it as needed to make it not so sticky (yet still soft). I kneaded it until I could stretch a ball of it out to be translucent (the windowpane test) without it tearing.

I set it aside to rise in the fridge. Again, an overnight rise would have been great.

When I was ready for the rest of the recipe, I pulled the dough out of the fridge first. It had risen up nicely. I punched it down and cut it into halves, which I formed into small balls. I set these aside to proof (rise) and to come up to room temperature.

Then I started up the coals, and as soon as they were ready, I put the Dutch ovens (remember, I did two) on 20-plus coals each. I put the sausage in and browned it, separating it into small chunks as I went. While I was doing that, I was also chopping up the onions, peppers, and other fillings.

I also got some more coals started and put about 20 hot coals on each lid to begin preheating.

Once the sausage was browned, I scooped it out. I added a little bit of garlic powder, salt, and olive oil to the Dutch oven and spread that around the bottom. That and the sausage flavoring would give the crust a great taste! I stretched out the dough, pretty evenly, and spread it over the bottom of the Dutch oven. I tried to press it up the sides as much as possible, but it didn't really respond. I took a fork and poked holes in the crust about every inch or so. I'm still not sure why the research I'd done said to do that, but almost every recipe had mentioned it, so I did it too.

The instructions said to "parbake" the crust, or, in other words, to bake it a bit before you add the fillings and bake it for real. At the time I wasn't sure why you would do that, but later I realized that there is going to be a lot of food on the crust. It will be thick and heavy. In order for that bottom crust to stand up, it needs to have some poof and structure first.

So, after the crust was spread, I put the heated lid on and put about 8 coals below and 18 coals above. I let that bake for only a few minutes. I would recommend checking it after 10–12 minutes. The crust should be a bit firm, but not browned. While that was baking, I made the sauce. The sauce was easy, I just mixed everything (except the mozzarella) and blended it to taste in a bowl.

Then, I took the Dutch ovens off the heat and put the fillings of choice in each one. I started with a layer of the mozzarella and then just added everything else. In each one, I did cubed ham, pepperoni, and the sausage I'd cooked. I actually quartered the pepperoni slices too, to make them more like chunks. In one, then, I added onions and peppers, and in the other I put the spinach and the tomatoes. I kept the fillings away from the edge of the crust.

Then, I stretched out the remaining dough balls and laid them on top. I reached under and pinched the two crusts together, all around the circle. I pressed on the top to kind of spread it back out to the edge of the Dutch oven.

Once these Dutch ovens were ready, I put the coals on and under them and let the ovens bake, turning them from time to time. I let the pizzas bake for 15–20 minutes and then checked them. They were turning a bit brown. I poured the remaining sauce over the entire tops of the pizzas and layered on a mountain of shredded mozzarella. I let them bake for another 15–20 minutes. At that point, they should be done and ready.

In the end, they tasted great.

# Spanish (Spain)

## PAELLA

This recipe all began one day with me being a couch potato, a dud spud surfing the channels. Bored of home-shopping TV and infomercials, I turned to my DVR and noticed that I had managed to acquire a few more episodes of Alton Brown's *Good Eats*.

One of the episodes was about a Spanish dish called "paella" (which is pronounced "pie-AY-yah"). I'd seen recipes for this many times but had never thought to try it. It required a special pan, also called a paella, and it was cooked outdoors over coals. That got me thinking.

I watched the episode a couple of times, and I was intrigued. It had several techniques and ingredients I had never tried before. Were those ingredients absolutely necessary? Could the techniques be adapted to a Dutch oven?

I called my expert sister and asked for a second opinion. She confirmed that, yes, in order to make a really good paella, you really did need special rice and good Spanish saffron (the expensive stuff). She was skeptical about doing it in a pan that was not a paella, however. I decided to give it a try anyway.

I spent two weeks acquiring all of the various ingredients, rewatching the show, and planning my processes. In the end, it was well worth the effort!

**TOOLS**

8-inch Dutch oven
12–15 coals underneath

12-inch Dutch oven
20+ coals underneath

**INGREDIENTS**

6 cups chicken broth
olive oil
5–6 chicken thighs
1 red bell pepper
1 green bell pepper
1 yellow bell pepper
2–4 cloves garlic
½ lb. green beans
2 cups rice (short-grain Spanish or Italian)
salt and pepper
20 threads Spanish saffron
1 tsp. smoked paprika
1 tsp. kosher salt
rosemary
basil
oregano

pulp and juice from 1 large tomato
juice of ½ lemon
¼ cup chopped fresh parsley

**AS I** shopped around, I watched closely for the ingredients. Alton and my sister both recommended Valencia rice. I had a hard time finding that, but I ended up with a short-grain Italian rice called "arborio." Getting the saffron was even trickier. I shopped around and called stores, and found something in a store near me labeled "Spanish saffron." It seemed to meet all of the criteria that I'd been told, and cost about the same as what I'd been seeing in spice specialty shops, so I bought it. It was about 18 dollars for a gram or two. Pricey stuff.

On cooking day, the first step was to get some coals ready. One bunch of them went under my 8-inch Dutch oven, and another set went under my 12-inch. In the 8-inch, I put three frozen blocks of my own homemade chicken stock. Six cups. In the end I didn't need it all, but It was good to have it all there and ready. I put it on the coals so it would melt and heat up. It won't need to be used for quite a while, so if you're working with boxed or bottled stock, you can probably start heating it up much later in the process.

The 12-inch got a little bit of olive oil. Once it was heated I put in the chicken thighs, skin side down, to fry and brown. A lot of fat renders out of the skin. That's used as part of the dish along the way.

While the chicken was cooking, I diced up the peppers, minced the garlic, and snapped the beans. I also mixed the rice and the other dry seasonings in a bowl.

The tomato was done with an interesting process, taught by Alton. You want the tomato flavor, but without the seeds or the skin. I sliced the tomato across "the equator" and squeezed out the seeds. I got kind of lucky, as the tomatoes that I had bought were pretty large and pulpy. Then, I put the open face of the sliced tomato against my cheese grater and grated the pulp and the juice into a bowl. The more I grated, the flatter the skin became, and so I got more and more pulp. Clever. If you don't want to do this, you could probably just use a smaller can of crushed or diced tomatoes.

When the chicken was brown on both sides, I pulled it out of the Dutch oven. I tossed in the veggies and sprinkled in some salt. Once the veggies were going soft, I added the tomato pulp and let that cook for a bit. Finally, the rice and seasoning mix was stirred into the pot. I also used this opportunity to replenish my coals.

At that point, it was time to put it all together and do the final cooking. I put the chicken back in, nestling it down into the rice and veggie mixture. I ladled the now-simmering stock from the 8-inch oven into the 12-inch oven, until the rice was well covered. I let that cook, with the

lid off, watching occasionally as it went. Every 10–15 minutes or so, I would see that much of the liquid had been absorbed into the cooking rice, and I would ladle in a bit more stock. I was watching to see the rice become translucent. Occasionally, I used a spoon to check the deeper rice, and to taste. I was careful as I added more stock because I wanted enough for the rice to absorb but not so much for it to end up like a soup, or even a thick stew. I could see why it was important to have the stock preheated on the side, so I wasn't shocking it with cool liquid and having to heat it all back up to continue with the cooking.

As the end of the cooking time approached, I squeezed the lemon juice over the whole dish and sprinkled on the chopped parsley.

Finally, when the rice was translucent and soft, it came off the coals. I don't know how long it took to get there; I was paying more attention to the rice than the time. The last step was to let it rest with a kitchen towel on top. I'm not sure why it couldn't be covered with the Dutch oven lid. Perhaps the final resting time needs to be done with something porous on top so some moisture can escape. The final texture is moist and soft but not dripping with juice.

After 15–20 minutes in the resting phase (it could be even longer, if you want), it was time to serve it up. Since this was my first time making it, I didn't know how great paella was supposed to taste. I'm not certain if I got the right rice or the right saffron, but I think I did. Still, what I was eating was one of the most delicious meals I'd had in a long time. I guess that qualifies it as a success

# German

## SPAETZLE WITH ONIONS

In my never-ending quest for dishes from all over the world to cook in my American Dutch oven, I came across Spaetzle (pronounced "sh-pets-leh"). I first had the dish when it was cooked in the kitchen of my wife's cousin and best friend. She had spent some time in Munich, Germany. I truly loved the dish, and I got it in my head to try it out in a Dutch oven. I haven't done many dishes from northern or central Europe. I thought it would be fun to try.

I did a bit of research and discovered that the dish I had eaten was only one variation of millions of possibilities. Spaetzle is a sort of German pasta/dumpling, and they make it with a wide variety of sauces, fillings, and other things. It's mostly served as a side dish, actually.

But I still decided to do it mostly like I'd first encountered it. I say "mostly" because I can never leave anything alone.

This dish is really done in two steps.

## STEP ONE: THE SPAETZLE

### TOOLS

8-inch Dutch oven
15+ coals below

### INGREDIENTS

4–5 cups water
2½ cups flour
1 tsp. salt
½ tsp. (or a liberal shake of) nutmeg
5 eggs
½–1 cup water

**I STARTED** up the coals and put the 8-inch Dutch oven on them, with 4–5 cups of water in it. While that was heating and boiling, I mixed the flour, salt, and nutmeg and then added the eggs. Finally, I started adding the ½–1 cup of water a little bit at a time. I added a little, then stirred, then added, then stirred. My wife's cousin had said that it needs to be like an extra thick cake batter. I would recommend using around ¾ cup of water. Maybe a little more.

I'd read that there were two ways to make the spaetzle: One is to put the dough into a colander and press it through the holes. The other way is to have an actual spaetzle press (which is the method I used). I'm not sure which one would be easier or messier. The jury's still out.

But I held the press (or the colander) over some boiling water in the Dutch oven and pressed the batter through the holes. It dropped into the water and sank. When the water boiled up again and the spaetzle strings started floating a couple of minutes later, I let it boil for 3–5 minutes more and then fished them out with a slotted spoon. I drained them and set them aside. I'm told you can even put it all in the fridge for another day.

I did it in bits. I squeezed a bit of batter into the water, let it cook, pulled it out, and then did it again. Then I repeated it until all the batter is cooked. Now it's time for . . .

### STEP TWO: THE MAIN DISH

**TOOLS**
12-inch Dutch oven
8–10 coals below
16–18 coals above

**INGREDIENTS**
olive oil
2–3 medium onions, sliced or diced
2 Tbsp. minced garlic
the spaetzle
1 cup sliced fresh mushrooms
2–3 chopped green onions (including greens)
chopped fresh parsley
juice from 1 lemon
salt and pepper
3–4 links smoked sausage or bratwurst
2 handfuls grated mozzarella

**I STARTED** off with all the coals under the Dutch oven, with a little olive oil in it, and started sautéing the onions, garlic, spaetzle, and mushrooms. I let them sauté until they were a little brown. Then I added the green onions, parsley, lemon juice, and salt and pepper. One last stir.

Then I arranged the sausage lengths on top (I put them all on one side because my wife doesn't like sausage much). Finally, I topped it with the mozzarella.

Then I reset the oven on the coals as listed above and let it bake for about 20 minutes, enough to combine all the flavors, cook the sausage, and melt the cheese.

Finally, it was time to dish it up and serve! Spaetzle is essentially a pasta, but it's made totally differently from Italian noodles. The spaetzle noodles, the cheese, and the onions make for a lightly sweet undertone, and the sausage makes it savory and spicy. It's a delicious combination!

# French

## CHICKEN CORDON BLEU

This recipe is also a great story from early in my cooking life, so I'm going to pull it straight from the blog. It's all about me learning a fundamental skill.

## FEBRUARY 23, 2009

This last weekend, I got schooled.

That's okay, though; it was a good thing!

My father was in town (from Indiana), and he was visiting for a short time. Whenever he and/or Mom are here in Utah, we always get together with my sister and brother-in-law too. Well, I've mentioned before that they are both great chefs and have worked in restaurants and are just plain incredible cooks. Amazing.

Well, when we got together on Saturday for lunch, I started talking to my brother-in-law about cheffery and asking him about how to shop for knives. Somehow we get talking about sauces. I mentioned my disaster with the Alfredo sauce I tried to make. Then he talked me through the whole process, beginning with a roux.

The next day, since they were coming over for dinner, I decided to do a chicken cordon bleu recipe and to make a cheddar cheese sauce using his instructions.

Well, they came out in time to see me put it all together, and he stepped me through the process. So, now I can do cream sauces and thick cream soups without fear!

### TOOLS

12-inch Dutch oven
10 coals below
20 coals above (slightly less in warmer weather)

### INGREDIENTS

**Liberal shakes of**
salt
black pepper
crushed cayenne pepper (not quite so liberal)
thyme
sage

bowl with 1–2 cups of well-crushed bread crumbs

3–4 lbs. boneless chicken breasts (thawed)
1 brick mozzarella cheese, from which to cut slices
1 small block cured meat, from which to cut slices (usually ham, but this time I used pastrami—turkey pastrami, since my brother-in-law is Jewish and doesn't eat pork)

**I STARTED** by mixing all of the spices in the first set of ingredients into the bread crumbs on a paper plate. Then, I pounded a chicken breast until it was spread out and flat. I put a slice of mozzarella in the center, and then a pretty thick slice of pastrami over that. If you get your pastrami presliced, you'll probably want to fold over a couple of slices. Then I folded the edges of the pounded-out chicken over it. The cheese and the pastrami were small enough that I could fold the chicken around it and without having to secure it with a toothpick.

Then I picked it up, dredged it in the crumbs and spices, and put it into the bottom of an oiled Dutch oven. (As a sidenote, I used some of my chili-and-onion-flavored oil!)

I repeated this process with the other chicken breasts. I had a lot, so I ended up packing them in there pretty tight.

Then, I just took them out back and put them on the coals. I probably baked them for 40 minutes or so.

Sidenote: I also took my 10-inch Dutch oven and made some rice with some chicken stock, some lemon juice, and some chopped green onions (don't forget the salt and pepper).

## THE SAUCE

### TOOLS

8-inch Dutch oven
10–12 coals below

### INGREDIENTS

1 stick butter
½–¾ cup flour

1 cup milk
1 cup cream
sprinkle of nutmeg
about ½ cup grated cheddar cheese, maybe more
few pinches of salt

**WE STARTED** by making the roux. Now, there are lots of different kinds of roux. Some are runny, some are cooked longer and are darker, but the one my bro-in-law taught me was thick and light.

First, he had me put a full stick of butter in the 8-inch Dutch oven, on the coals. Once it had melted, we added a bit more than ½ cup of flour and stirred it with a whisk. It almost had the consistency of sugar cookie dough. It would hold together as I was stirring it, but then would slowly flatten out when I stopped. I cooked it until it was a little darker than when it started, but still blond.

We pulled that completely out of the Dutch oven and set it aside in a bowl. Since we didn't know just how thick we wanted the sauce to be, we were going to add it in later.

Then we put in the milk and the cream and set it to boil, with the nutmeg sprinkled in. Once it was boiling, we started adding roux, maybe a little under a tablespoon at a time, stirring it in with the whisk. In no time, we'd found the magic amount to get the right thickness (2–3 tablespoons).

Then, as it boiled again, we added the cheese. This time, the cheese melted and bonded with the flour, and it made a great sauce. It didn't "break" and end up in a coagulated clump in the bottom of the Dutch oven. We added some salt to taste, and away we went! We also added some of the chicken stock from the bottom of the cordon bleu Dutch oven! Yum!

The chicken (and the rice) would have been great by themselves, but that sauce took it to a whole new level. It made the meal! And it was simple.

And then, my brother-in-law explained some other things—including, with that same base but with more milk, and sautéed mushrooms, onions, and celery, you have cream of mushroom soup! With tomatoes, you have cream of tomato soup! With asiago and parmesan cheese, instead of cheddar, you have Alfredo sauce. And so on, and so on. Sauces and soups from the same base. Amazing!

I also served it with some sourdough bread. It was the tastiest chicken cordon bleu recipe I'd tasted, and it was certainly the best one I'd ever made.

It also goes to show that learning to cook in a Dutch oven is really all about learning to cook, in a Dutch oven.

## FRENCH BREAD

The first time I tried to do French bread, I didn't blog about it because, frankly, it was good but not *that* good.

I was kinda proud of myself for making the attempt. Making good French bread is intimidating to me. I mean, when I'm doing my sourdough, or my sandwich loaves, there are a lot of enriching ingredients there to aid in the leavening and the flavor. In some ways, they're like crutches. You can mess up a little bit and it'll still be okay because the sugar will make it sweet and help it rise, the egg and milk will help make it fluffy, and so on.

But with French bread, you get none of that. It's just flour, yeast, water, and salt. And that's it. And you have to make magnificent, delicious, fluffy bread, with a rich brown crust with nothing more than that.

If *that* doesn't scare you, then you have no clue what you're up against!

Or, at least, that's what I kept telling myself.

But I have two great teachers in my corner. One is Peter Reinhart and his book *The Bread Baker's Apprentice*. The other is the great lady that gave me the book for Christmas, my dear sister!

So I used Peter's recipe and procedure as best I could the first time I made it, and then, after talking to my sister, I applied her techniques as well. The problem with Reinhart is that he's cooking the bread in nice commercial ovens, not in a charcoal-heated Dutch oven in a backyard. So I had to adapt his procedures somewhat. My sister helped me with that.

Another thing that I learned along the way is that bread is a process, not a recipe. That's really true of almost all dishes, but bread more so. The more you learn of the process, the better your bread will be.

Reinhart's French bread is done in three stages. One batch of dough is made and ferments overnight. It's blended with a second one that ferments on the kitchen counter. Finally it's shaped and proofed and baked.

The first stage is called the pâte fermentée. (Don't ask me how to pronounce it; I'm a hick from a small town in Utah.)

## PÂTE FERMENTÉE

### INGREDIENTS

½ tsp. yeast
1 cup water

2¼ cups bread flour
¾ tsp. salt
flour for kneading

**I STARTED** by mixing the yeast and the water. Reinhart suggests using "instant" yeast, but I didn't have any, so I still activated my regular yeast in the water. It doesn't foam up like it would if there were sugar in the water, so I just dissolved it.

Then I mixed the flour and the salt in a bowl and then poured in the water and yeast mix. I stirred that up and started to knead it. I shook in a little flour as I went, but not much. I found the texture to be very different than the enriched breads I'd done before. It was more like play-dough. It took a little getting used to.

I did knead it a good while, but I didn't do a windowpane test. It seemed to me that I'd be adding it to the other dough and re-kneading it the next day anyway.

After the kneading, I put it back in the bowl (oiled) and let it sit under plastic wrap for about an hour. It did rise, but it didn't balloon up like the other breads I've done. Then I put it in the fridge to continue fermenting overnight.

The first time I attempted this, I didn't do the overnight thing. I did this step, let it rise for about 2 hours total, and then moved on to step two. I think that when I have time, I'm definitely recommending the overnight rise. Like Reinhart says, more fermenting time develops flavor.

## THE DOUGH

### TOOLS

12-inch shallow Dutch oven
12 coals below
25 coals above

### INGREDIENTS

½ tsp. yeast
1 cup water (at about 100 degrees)

pâte fermentée from the night before
2½ cups bread flour
¾ tsp. salt

**THE NEXT** day, I mixed the yeast and the water, to activate the yeast. I took the pâte fermentée out of the fridge and let it come up in temperature as much as possible. I cut it into 10–12 pieces. I mixed the flour and the salt, and added the pâte fermentée. Finally, I added the yeast and the water. I used a pastry cutter, at first, to cut and mix the dough, and then I just used my hands.

I turned it out onto my floured tabletop and started kneading. It took quite a while to pass the windowpane test (when you can stretch a small dough ball out to be translucent without it tearing). When that was all done, I put it back in that (oiled) bowl and set it aside to rise for about 2 hours.

When it had risen well, I took it out and shaped it into a boule (that's French for "ball"). Even as I was shaping it, I was trying to not be too rough so as to not degas (remove gas from) it as much as possible. I set it aside, under plastic wrap, for its final proof. If I'd had any baking parchment, I would have set it aside on a sheet, and then on a plate, because, well, you'll see.

Right away, I went out and got some coals burning. I was going to preheat the entire oven this time, rather than just the lid. It took a while for the coals to fire up, but they did, and I put 12 coals underneath the Dutch oven and about 25 above. That should make it somewhere around 475 degrees. I let it heat up for about 15 minutes or so.

While that was heating and the dough was still proofing, I gathered up a few more tools. I got a spritz bottle of water, a paring knife, and my meat thermometer.

Now here's the technique my sister told me about. She said to do these following steps quickly, in about as much time as it takes to explain it. So, I did.

I dropped the boule of dough into the now-hot Dutch oven. I sliced the top of the dough three times. I spritzed it with water a few times. I stuck in the thermometer. I closed the lid.

Okay, actually, the thermometer is my idea, not my sister's or Reinhart's. I just can never tell when bread is done, so I use the thermometer and cook it to an internal temperature of 190–200 degrees. The spritz is what Reinhart and my sister both say helps to form the famous French bread crust. It also helps with the "spring" to help the bread get really big in the oven. Had I used the parchment, I could have lowered the boule in much more smoothly and lost less gas and body in the process. I'll do that next time (you should do it every time).

I probably cooked it for 30–45 minutes. I kept adding a few fresh coals and turning the lid and the body of the Dutch oven every 15 minutes or so. I don't cook to time, but rather to temperature.

Then, I pulled it off the coals and let it cool. It tasted great. It was a large loaf, and the crumb was light. The crust was crunchy as well. It was good enough for me to declare it a true winner.

## BRENDON'S CRÈME BRÛLÉE

I love it when I have a culinary victory. There are dishes that defeated me at first but which I later conquered. I like to be able to come back to a total flop and have it turn out great. It makes me feel like I'm actually learning something. Often, when I come back a third time, it's even better.

I included this recipe for my son Brendon. Several times now he's tried to do a crème brûlée, but each time it didn't turn out quite the way we wanted. Once it was a bit bland and strangely gray in color. Another time it didn't set and was almost completely liquid. Finally, we took a little time and did it together. Actually, he did it, with only minimal observation and input from me. And it worked!

This recipe is based on one from *America's Test Kitchen*. It's a little bit different, simplified in the process from so many others we looked up, and adapted for the Dutch oven.

We also had to shop around some to find ramekins. Those are the small, shallow ceramic dishes for desserts like, well, crème brûlée. It was tricky to buy them because we wondered how many we would be able to fit into the Dutch oven. The small, deep, round ones would easily fit seven, but the larger, shallower ovals would only fit four.

You'll also need a blowtorch. Yes, I said that right. We borrowed a small plumber's torch from a neighbor. You can go out and spend about thirty dollars for a small kitchen torch. That's a bit too much to spend on a unitasker in my mind.

### TOOLS

12-inch Dutch oven
Part 1: 20+ coals below
Part 2: 13–14 coals below, 13–14 coals above

several 4- to 5-oz. ceramic ramekins

### INGREDIENTS

water

6 large egg yolks

2 cups heavy cream
⅓ cup sugar
pinch of salt
1 tsp. vanilla extract
shake of cinnamon
shake of nutmeg

brown sugar to sprinkle and melt on top
mint leaves to garnish, if desired

**TO START,** we got some coals lit. While those were catching on, we put the ramekins in the Dutch oven and poured water in around them, about ¾ of the way up the sides of the ramekins. Then we removed them and set them aside. When the coals were ready, we spread them around and set the Dutch oven on top, with the lid on, to let the water boil.

Then we turned our attention to the custard itself. Brendon began by separating the egg yolks from the whites. While Jacob, his assistant, whisked the yolks, Brendon mixed the other (third set) ingredients together in a bowl. Finally, while whisking, Brendon slowly combined the yolks with the cream mix. A few final whisks, and it was done.

The mix was then poured into the ramekins and evened out between them all.

Soon after, the water was at a nice even boil, and Brendon gently set the ramekins into the water. It was kinda tricky, but wearing leather gloves helped. We put the lid back on and adjusted the coals to be on the bottom and the top, as listed.

We let it cook for 35–40 minutes. Occasionally we'd check the set of the custard and the temperature. You want to cook it to 170–175 degrees and until the centers are jiggly but not sloshy.

We pulled the oven off the coals and pulled out the ramekins, letting them cool on a rack. Once they'd cooled a bit, Brendon put them in the fridge to chill. They continued to set a bit as they cooled and even more as they chilled.

After our dinner, brimming with excitement, Brendon fetched the ramekins and the torch. This final step isn't correctly done unless it's performed in front of the diners. He sprinkled a little bit of brown sugar atop each one and fired it up. (What is it about young boys and fire?) Keeping the torch moving, he melted the sugar into a crust. Then he sprinkled on some mint and served them to our guests, proud as can be.

It was delicious. And we chalked up another victory!

# Hungarian

## MARK'S GOULASH

This dish is more of an American version of a traditional eastern European stew. I still think it tastes great, though. Remember what I said early on about authenticity?

When you're looking for something to cook with some ground beef or some stew meat, and you're not sure what, you really can't go wrong with goulash. It's easy and tasty. In this case, I happened to have a pound of stew meat wrapped up and frozen, and I thought I'd use it. I just did a few Net searches to get an idea of what to put in, and this is what I came up with.

### TOOLS

12-inch Dutch oven
15–20 coals below

### INGREDIENTS

oil
2 medium onions
2 stalks celery
4 cloves garlic
salt

1 lb. stew beef (or ground beef)

1–2 cups chicken stock
1 (15.25-oz.) can corn, drained
2 (8-oz.) cans tomato sauce
oregano
basil
salt
pepper

1 lb. bag of egg noodles

**More optional ingredients to consider in the third step:**
paprika (the stronger stuff—this is required in real goulash)
crushed red peppers
a bit of milk or cream (like a quarter or half cup)

**I JUST** started off with a lot of coals underneath my 12-inch Dutch oven, with a little oil in the bottom (maybe a tablespoon's worth, or a capful). While that was getting good and hot, I sliced up the onions and the celery and minced the garlic. Once the Dutch oven was hot, I dropped the first set of ingredients in and sautéed them.

Here's a hint, by the way, about onions. Don't store them outside or in your garage in the winter. They partly freeze, so they don't sauté and caramelize well. Not that I would ever do that. Nope. Not me. But now you know!

Once the onions were as done as they were gonna get, I moved them aside and put the meat in to brown.

Step three was to add everything else (except the noodles). At that point, it was all pretty runny, more like a soup. I was a bit nervous, actually. I considered adding some kind of flour or other thickener but decided to wait and see what would happen after the noodles cooked. That turned out to be a wise choice.

Finally, I added the noodles and covered it up. By the time the noodles were al dente (10–15 minutes or so), they had absorbed much of the liquid and it was a nice, thick goulash. The family loved it!

# Russian

## COULIBIAC

One year, I got four cookbooks for Christmas. Most of them were the big, hefty 500-plus pagers with all kinds of recipes in them. One was a really cool book all about breads. More on that in another book. Another one had a lot of fancier dishes, with beautiful full-color photos.

Well, one week, I looked in the pantry and the freezer to see what we had and saw some salmon fillets in the freezer. So, I started looking for ways to "do salmon." I looked through the books, and I found a bunch of recipes for various marinades and sauces, and they all sounded good.

Then, I stumbled across one called "coulibiac." I'd never heard of it. I didn't even know how to pronounce it. (It's "koo-leeb-yahk". I Googled it.) The thought of salmon and rice and tomatoes all in a pastry shell got me really excited! It was a totally new way (for me) to look at fish. In the coulibiac, the fish is a part of the dish, as flavor and texture, rather than the whole center of the dish itself.

I did it in two days. I'm glad I did because I ran into some real troubles with the pastry. The recipe calls for "puff pastry" as the shell. At the time, I didn't know what that was, so I looked it up in the back of the book. It directed me to a recipe for what it called "puff pastry"—something to make cream puffs and éclairs. I made a batch of it and was really frustrated when it ended up as a batter, not as a crust. I tried again, thinking I had misinterpreted and mismeasured. Not so. Now I had two bowls of goop that were both clearly unusable for what I was trying.

So I dove into the book. I looked up every possible variation of "puff pastry" I could think of. Finally, I just looked up pies, and there was an aside about all kinds of different pie crusts, one of which, you guessed it, was called "puff pastry"!

So, I made a couple of batches of that and chilled it overnight.

The next day, I rolled out the pastry, added the filling, and baked it. But that will all come out in the recipe's instructions.

Also, I made a double batch of the filling, thinking I would make two coulibiacs. It turns out that the basic recipe already makes enough for two, so the recipe below is plenty. But I had to double the crust recipe. Actually, I mixed it and rolled it out twice. Also, I combined some of the steps to make it easier to cook in the Dutch oven. Even with that, though, it ended up looking and tasting quite gourmet. And when you bring it out to the table and pronounce it correctly, you're sure to impress! It will serve a lot of people because it's very filling.

**TOOLS**
12-inch Dutch oven (reused in two steps)
step one: 12 coals above, 12 coals below (I used more, 'cause it was winter)
step two: 21 coals above, 12 coals below (425 degrees. Again, I used more, 'cause it was winter)

## STEP ONE:

### THE FILLING

**INGREDIENTS**
⅓ cup rice
⅓ cup chicken broth or water
1–2 medium onions, diced
4 Tbsp. butter, in cubes or slices
1 (14-oz.) can diced tomatoes, undrained
2 lbs. salmon
juice of one lemon
zest of one lemon
liberal shakes of salt, black pepper, parsley
not-so-liberal shakes of chili powder (just to add a little zip, not to heat it up)

**I STARTED** by heating up come coals and adding all the ingredients to a 12-inch Dutch oven. I assembled it in layers, but it all ends up being mixed together, so I don't know that it's absolutely necessary. The salmon, after it's cooked, will break up in the stirring. I put the rice and the broth in first, then the onions and the butter. I used butter slices so that it would melt and blend better, rather than getting a big butter spot in the middle. Then came the tomatoes. I layered the salmon (it was frozen) on top of that, and put the spices and the lemon juice on last.

Once that was on the coals, it only took 30–40 minutes to cook. The salmon cooks fast, but the rice takes a little longer. It also takes some time to get the Dutch oven up to temperature, especially on a cold January day.

While that was cooking, I started on the crust. Here's where I had my frustrating misadventures with the éclair batter. As I mentioned, I ended up making two batches of this recipe, for two (side-by-side) coulibiacs.

### THE CRUST

**INGREDIENTS**
2 cups flour
6 Tbsp. butter
6 Tbsp. shortening
dash of lemon juice

**I COMBINED** all the ingredients in a bowl and mixed them with a pastry knife. I put that on my floured counter and rolled it out. It was still pretty sticky at that point. I rolled it not so wide, and more long. Then, I folded it bottom up and top down, in thirds. I sprinkled more flour on the countertop and rolled it out again. I repeated this several times, turning the dough each time. Finally, after three or four foldings/rollings, I put each batch of dough on a plate, wrapped it in plastic, and popped it in the fridge.

By that time, the salmon mix should be done for you. I pulled it out of the Dutch oven and put it in a big mixing bowl. Since there are tomatoes in the recipe, I didn't want to leave it in the Dutch oven and ruin my seasoning patina. Then I covered the bowl up and put it in the fridge. In winter, we have a really big fridge that doubles in the summer as a garage.

**STEP TWO:**

The next day, I rolled out the dough. The original recipe said to roll it into a square, about 11 × 16. I didn't measure, but I shot for that size. Then I put a lot of the filling in the middle. I cracked open a couple of eggs and beat them. I rolled the filling up, burrito-style, sealing the seams with the beat-up egg along the way. I would also recommend cutting a wedge out of each "corner" so that the crust doesn't get so thick from folding over.

The recipe suggested cutting a few strips of crust dough off before you roll it up to use as decoration, either twisted or braided. I decided to go for the extra style points and try that. It really made it look cooler. Traditionally, you're also supposed to cut some stylish holes in it, much like you do in an apple pie, which will let the steam vent.

I did that for both coulibiacs and then put them side-by-side (kinda crowded) into my 12-inch Dutch oven. With both of them in the oven, I coated them each in more beaten egg. I put that oven onto the coals and baked it for about 1 hour. That's longer than the recipe called for, but it's an indoor recipe, and I was dealing with cold weather and heating up the cast iron.

I turned the Dutch oven a lot, every 15–20 minutes, to make sure that it didn't burn on the bottom. When it was all hot and the crust was a rich brown, I pulled it off. It was done!

I sliced it meatloaf style into about two-inch slices. The book suggested a drizzle of melted butter, garlic, and lemon juice, so I tried that. It was nice, but it was already pretty rich, so I'm not sure it needed it. My wife suggested that it would have also tasted great drizzled with a Newburg sauce. Hmmmm . . .

Nonetheless, this one was a delicious treat, and quite the impressive visual as well. Kinda swanky for a back-porch kitchen, eh?

# LATIN AMERICA

## Mexican

The Dutch oven is an integral part of the history of the American southwest, which many years ago used to be a part of Mexico. After the Mexican-American war, in the 1840s, Mexico lost almost a million square miles to the United States, covering areas in the states that are now California, Arizona, Utah, New Mexico, Texas, Nevada, and parts of Colorado, Kansas, and Oklahoma (where the wind comes sweeping down the plain).

At the time, the cowboys of the Old West used the Dutch oven on their cattle drives, and the prospectors used them in their mining camps. It's no surprise that so much of the Mexican cuisine is still a part of American southwest food, and how easily it translates to the Dutch oven.

### MARK'S CHICKEN TAMALES

Many years ago, when we lived in West Jordan, Utah, there was this Mexican family that lived down the street. I don't recall all their names, but one of the young boys was named Miguel. He'd come by and say hi occasionally.

His *abuelita* moved up from Agua Prieta (in the north of Mexico) if I recall correctly. She was a nice lady, and once every few months she would take a couple of days and make pots and pots of tamales.

Now, I liked tamales, but this lady made tamales like there was no tamale! They were the most incredible I'd ever tasted. And she would send Miguel and his sisters door-to-door with five-gallon buckets full of these corn-wrapped delicacies, selling them for a buck apiece. We'd always get as many as we had cash for, sometimes up to twenty.

I was told you could freeze them, but they never lasted that long at our house.

That family ended up moving. Ever since then, I've been on a quest to find the perfect tamale. No restaurant has ever equaled the magnificence of la Maestra de la Cocina.

Of course, I also had to try my hand at making tamales. At first, I wanted someone to show me how. That would be cool. But scheduling and everything is just too tough. But once, while we were in San Diego, we had some tamales in a restaurant that were almost, but not quite, half as good as the ones I remembered. It was then that I determined that tamales would be my next Dutch oven project.

Immediately, I began my research. I bought a steaming rack that would fit in the Dutch oven. I bought the corn husk sheaves. I was ready, and I made my first batch of fifteen to eighteen tamales. I didn't count.

Oh, they were delicious. I'm biased, so I'm not sure I can claim if I got it close or not.

### TOOLS

several Dutch ovens (I used my 12-inch shallow, my 12-inch deep, and my 8-inch)
lots and lots of coals below and about 10 or so on top, depending on the stage of the project
steamer rack

### INGREDIENTS

#### The Filling

3–4 lbs. boneless chicken (I used frozen chicken tenderloins. You can use pork or beef too.)
about 6 cups water
1 medium onion, sliced and quartered
1 heaping tsp. chopped garlic
4 bay leaves
2 Tbsp. salt
about 30 whole black peppercorns
2–3 tsp. dried oregano, plus more for later
3 Tbsp. ground cumin, plus more for later

4–6 Tbsp. flour (added later)

20–30 dried corn husks (hojas) to wrap the masa and the filling (you'll need 1 or 2 for each tamale)

**The Masa (Dough)**
4 cups masa harina flour
2 tsp. baking powder
2½ cups broth from cooking the filling (see below)
1½ cups shortening

**FIRST I** made the filling. To start with, I put the frozen chicken into the Dutch oven. (I originally did it in my 12-inch shallow. I could have saved some cleaning and done it all in my 12-inch deep, but I didn't). Then I added the other ingredients for the filling, except the flour. I put that pot on a lot of coals (probably 20 or so), covered it, and let it start boiling. After about 45 minutes, the chicken was boiled, and it was smelling really good.

I brought it in and used a straining spoon to lift the chicken and the onion out of the Dutch oven. I shredded the chicken into a bowl with a couple of forks, then sprinkled some of the broth back onto it. Onto that, I sprinkled the flour and stirred it up, which gave it a bit of thickness and also shredded the chicken up a little bit more. I also added a bit more of the cumin powder, oregano, and a bit of ground black pepper. Not too much—just some sprinkles to replace what was settling in the bottom of the Dutch oven.

Now if I were in more of a hurry, I'd have been soaking the corn husks (hojas) in hot water while I was cooking the meat. But, then again, if I were in a hurry, I wouldn't have been making tamales in a Dutch oven, now, would I? So, at this point, I put the hojas on to soak and started to mix the masa.

The masa was easy to make: I put all the ingredients into a bowl. There really are only two special instructions. At the bottom of the Dutch oven I used to cook the meat, the spices had settled to the bottom. When I dipped out the broth to mix in the masa, I tried not to disturb it so as to get a clearer broth. I did pick up some of the spices and powders, but not too much. The other thing I did was to get out a pastry cutter/mixer to blend it all. I guess you could just mix in the shortening by hand, but the pastry cutter worked really well.

Once the masa was mixed, and the hojas of corn husk were softened,

I started making tamales. I have to confess that I've never watched this done, I've only read about it, so my technique is not necessarily authentic. Nonetheless, it worked. I laid out a single hoja with the pointed end toward me. I spread a small ball of masa out so that it covered about a 2½-inch square toward the top of the hoja. Then, I spread out a 1-inch-wide line of meat filling from the top to the bottom in the middle of the masa. Then, I folded the right-hand side of the hoja over the filling and pulled the corn husk back. I folded the left side over, held the hoja there, and refolded the right hand hoja back over, wrapping the masa and the filling up in corn husk hoja. Then, I folded the point up into a nice tamale envelope. I did this with each corn husk hoja and stacked them aside.

When I'd made all the tamales, I put the steamer rack into the 12-inch deep Dutch oven and put water in the bottom up to the level of the rack. I started to stack the tamales in the oven, on the steamer, so that the open end of the tamales was up. This was kinda tricky, since they didn't always want to stack. Still, I managed to get them all in. If I'd made more of them, I'd have been able to stack them all the way up against the walls of the Dutch oven. As it stood, the recipe didn't make enough to do that. There was plenty of meat, but I'd have had to make more masa. I decided to cook what I had and test it, rather than risk making a bigger disaster.

This Dutch oven, now covered, went out on some fresh coals. I put 18–20 coals underneath, packed in well, like the tamales were. Another 10 or so coals went on top, around the outer rim. Within about 15 minutes, I could start to see steam coming out of the edges of the lid. I steamed them for about 1 hour, refreshing the coals once. I only opened the lid once, and that was just to make sure that they were all still standing up and that all was well.

Finally, after that hour, I pulled one out, cooled it, and tasted it! Wow! It was great.

Also, in my 8-inch, I made a milder version of an enchilada sauce that I'd made previously.

**TOOLS**
8-inch Dutch oven
12 coals below

**INGREDIENTS**
3 Tbsp. oil

3 Tbsp. flour
2½ cups water
2 Tbsp. chili powder (this is where the "enchilada" part comes in)
1 Tbsp. garlic
salt to taste (about 1 Tbsp.)

**I STARTED** by heating the oil and the flour into a roux in the 8-inch Dutch oven (I still had plenty of coals left over) and then adding the remaining ingredients once the roux was browned. Those I stirred and simmered for about another 20 minutes, until it cooked down and thickened.

Finally, you unpeel three or so tamales, spoon on some sauce, and enjoy. Wow!

## RED PORK TAMALES

The next time I did tamales, I did it in two days. The night before, I cooked the pork, and then the next morning I made the filling and rolled the tamales. That evening, I set them in my Dutch oven and steamed them up! These were different from the last time I did them, both in process and in the recipe.

### TOOLS

**For the Pork Roast:**
12-inch deep Dutch oven
12–13 coals below
13–14 coals above

**For the Tamales:**
12-inch deep Dutch Oven, with a veggie steamer
25–30 coals underneath

### INGREDIENTS

**The Pork**
2–2½ lbs. pork roast
1 head garlic, cut into a few big chunks
1 Tbsp. black peppercorns
8 cups water
4–6 large bay leaves
1 tsp. salt

**The Filling**
6 oz. dried red chilies (pick your picante)
hot water
2 Tbsp. cilantro

4–5 cloves garlic, minced
2 cups pork stock, from the previous step
2 Tbsp. oil
2–4 Tbsp. flour
1 tsp. salt

**The Masa**
4 cups masa flour
4 cups pork stock, from the first step
2 tsp. baking powder
1 tsp. salt
1⅓ cups shortening

**I STARTED** with the pork. It's fairly simple; I just added all of the ingredients in the middle of my Dutch oven and roasted it. Braised it, really. In this case, I put on about 26 coals, 13 on the bottom and 13 on the top, and roasted it to the right temperature—160 degrees. Cooking it longer makes it come off the bone and come apart easier.

Once it's all done, I pulled the meat out of the Dutch oven. Then, using forks, I pulled it off the bone and pulled it apart into shreds.

What's left in the Dutch oven is very important stuff. Don't throw it away. Instead, I strained out all of the meat and spice particles and set aside the pork stock for the next day. I found there wasn't much fat to skim off, but if there had been I would have skimmed it. All of that stuff went into the fridge.

The next day, I got started pretty early. I crushed up the chilies (I used anchos, I think) and soaked them for 20–30 minutes in some hot water. Once they were soft, I strained them and added them, with the cilantro and the garlic, to the stock. I put all of that into a blender and whirred it all up.

Once that was all pureed, I strained it through a paper towel filter, so I just had the mash, and most of the runny liquid was drained.

At this point, I cheated (for those who may be purist Dutch oven chefs): I did a little work on my stovetop inside. In my defense, however, I did use a cast-iron skillet! I made a roux out of the oil and flour, and when that started to get a little bit past tan, I added in the strained mushed chilies mix. I cooked that for just a little bit, until it really started smelling rich, and then mixed it up with the pulled pork from the previous day, along with a teaspoon of salt. That made the filling, and it went back into the fridge.

Really, this could have easily been done in an 8- or 10-inch Dutch oven over about 12 coals.

Then, I turned my attention to the masa. This was pretty easy to make. I simply added all of the ingredients to a bowl and stirred it up using a pastry cutter. Done. You can adjust how moist it is by adding more masa flour or stock.

Now came the rolling phase. A disclaimer, by the way: I'm not a Mexican grandmother, and I've never seen one roll tamales, so I don't know if my method is "traditional" or "authentic." It worked, though. I did this pretty much the same way as I did in the previous recipe (method starts at bottom of page 101).

I put the veggie steamer into the 12-inch deep Dutch oven and unfolded it. I added water up to the level of the steamer and stacked the rolled tamales on the steamer. Then I put the oven out on the coals. I kept it to bottom heat, 25–30 coals. You're boiling it, so you'll want it to come to a boil fairly quickly. Then you can reduce the coals just to keep it simmering.

You may need to add water from time to time, since the total cook time for me was almost 2 hours. If you don't pay attention to that, they can end up drying out. Not good.

They were different than the previous tamales. I loved the spicy picante tones of the filling and the savory undertone of the masa.

## MOLE-STYLE ROAST

One day, I wanted to do something *different* . . . but I didn't know what.

That's nothing new, really. I find myself in that position a lot. I want to cook, but I don't know what I have ingredients for, I don't know what I'm up against, and so on. I do like to push myself, though. That's one reason why I love to do the challenges with Andy over at backporchgourmet.com. More on challenges later in the book!

In the end, I thought about chocolate. I wanted to try using chocolate in a savory-toned dish. I've done chocolate brownies, chocolate cakes, and chocolate cookies. But it's all sweet. Never have I done a savory chocolate meal.

Three nationalities really know how to do chocolate—one is the Mexicans, one is the Dutch, and one is the Swiss (I loves me my Toblerone). With the savory in my head, my mind went instantly to mole.

As I looked at various mole recipes online, I found a lot of things in common, and, as I expected, a lot of things were different. There really *is* a lot of things you can do and still call it a mole. And really, I wasn't so much wanting a *true* and *traditional* mole. For example, almost all of the meats I'd seen in mole recipes were chicken or pork. I could have done that, sure, but I had this small beef roast that I wanted to try. I didn't see any beef mole recipes. Maybe they're out there, maybe not.

So I didn't know if I was supposed to be able to do beef or not, but I did.

I also thought it would be cool to do the roast medium rare. I'm not sure why I wanted it that way. Maybe it just sounded fancier. In the end, it ended up rare, because of a bad calibration on my thermometer (see next page). So make sure that your thermometer measures accurately. It truly tasted great, though.

## TOOLS

12-inch Dutch oven
20+ coals below, and then
14 coals above and 12 coals below

8-inch Dutch oven
6–7 coals below

## INGREDIENTS

**The Roast**
1 (2- to 3-lb.) beef roast
salt
pepper
2–4 Tbsp. olive oil, divided

**The Mole Sauce**
¼ tsp. black pepper
cayenne pepper to taste
½ tsp. paprika
½ tsp. salt
½ tsp. ground cinnamon
1 tsp. brown sugar
½ cup beef broth (you might want more)
2 (1-oz.) cubes semisweet chocolate
2 Tbsp. raisins or dried cranberries, finely chopped
½ (3-oz) can tomato paste

**I STARTED** off by lighting up some coals. As they were getting white, I seasoned both sides of the well-thawed roast with plenty of salt and pepper. This was set aside to soak into the meat.

When the coals were hot, I put 1–2 tablespoons of olive oil in the inside of the 12-inch Dutch oven and set it on top of the coals to preheat, and to season a bit. After a while, I added 1–2 more tablespoons of olive oil to it and let that heat to shimmery. I laid the roast in and seared it for a few minutes on each side, to get some good caramelization going. Once that was done, I adjusted the coals for the roasting and relaxed.

After about 45 minutes, it was time to make the mole sauce. The mole sauce was simply a matter of mixing the ingredients in the 8-inch oven and putting it on the coals. I let it simmer slowly, melting the chocolate and combining the flavors. While the roast was still cooking, I spread a coating of the sauce on.

I carefully watched the temperature of the roast. When the internal temperature got to 140 degrees, I took it off the coals but left it in the Dutch oven. The residual heat of the Dutch oven will bring the temperature up to 145–150 degrees, which is a nice, comfortable medium doneness.

I served it with veggies on the side and a drizzle of more sauce on top, to the rave reviews of my children. I know it's good when they give me the thumbs up!

## Calibrating Thermometers

To calibrate your thermometer (or at least test it), you'll need some way to get a constant, certain temperature, and then you can check your thermometers against that. It turns out that water at sea level air pressure heats up until it gets to 212 degrees. Then it stops heating up, and it takes a lot of heat added into it to begin boiling and vaporizing. That means that if your water is boiling, it's at 212 degrees. Or, at least, it'll be close enough to get a cooking thermometer accurate.

If the thermometer's temperature is off, some have a nut under the dial that you can grab with a wrench and twist until the needle shows what you know the temperature is. It's calibrated. The ones I was using didn't have that, so I simply found that out of my four thermometers, one was way off. I threw it away.

## CHILE VERDE FOR CINCO DE MAYO

Some people would say Cinco de Mayo is more of an American holiday than a Mexican one. It's not even a mandatory Mexican national holiday. Originally, it celebrated a victory over the French at the battle of Puebla in the 1860s. Now it's a chance for Mexicans in America to celebrate their heritage. For a day we all get to be Mexican, or it's just like on St. Patrick's Day when we all get to be Irish.

At any rate, in my own attempt to be Mexican for a day, one May I made some chile verde. As usual, I gathered this recipe from a number of sources, mostly from the Web.

Whenever I have chile verde, I remember a time when we were foster parents. We were in a Mexican-American restaurant with one of the kids we were hosting at the time. He was of Mexican descent, probably second or third generation. He was getting all uptight about how inauthentic the food and atmosphere was and talking all about brown pride and "la raza." Then when he ordered it, he pronounced it like a gringo: "chil-ee vir-dee." He was a funny kid.

Also, the first time I did this, I'd been trying to figure out how to use chilies in my outdoor cooking. It seems to me that you can never fully tell just how spicy something's going to be just by how many jalapeños you add, right? I mean, the actual spiciness varies, it seems. I put in one chili one day, and wow! It's way too hot. Another day I put in three and it barely tickles. What's up with that?

Okay, I'm exaggerating. A little. But piquance is one of the flavor tones you have available, and it's easy to overdo. It's also easy to underdo it, to be too timid. One thing I've learned is to start slow and to creep up on the right level of spiciness. You can't take it out, but you can always add more, right?

I also like to do some black beans in my 10-inch oven and some rice in my 8-inch oven when I make this.

Anyway, here's the recipe I used. I don't know how "authentic" it is, but man was it tasty!

### TOOLS

12-inch shallow Dutch oven
20–22 coals below

10-inch Dutch oven
16–18 coals below

8-inch Dutch oven
12 coals below

**INGREDIENTS**
½ lb. black beans
4–5 cups water

1 yellow onion, chopped
2 Tbsp. minced garlic
2 Tbsp. olive oil
6 green onions, sliced (into the greens)

3 lbs. lean pork

3–4 cups water

8 large tomatillos, husk peeled and coarsely chopped
1 cup chicken stock

2–3 mild Anaheim chilies, sliced
1–3 jalapeños, sliced

2 tsp. oregano
2 tsp. ground sage
1½ tsp. ground cumin
¼ cup chopped fresh cilantro
juice of 1–2 lemons
½ tsp. salt (to taste)
¼ tsp. white pepper

sprinkles of flour, plus water, for thickening

1 cup rice
2 cups water (or even better, chicken stock)

**THE WHOLE** process started the night before when I took out a half pound of black beans and set them in a bowl to soak overnight. Completely cover the beans with water.

The next day, when cookin' time came, I started up some coals and, while they were getting ready, got the green and yellow onions and garlic chopped. I put the oil in the 12-inch Dutch oven and got it good and hot. I've learned that's the secret to sautéing. It's gotta be hot first.

While the onions were caramelizing, I cubed the pork and added that to brown in the same Dutch oven. Since the Dutch oven was quite hot, it was easy to get a good brown singe on the pork. Yummmm.

I don't remember exactly how or when, but somewhere in all that, I drained the water on the beans and put them in my 10-inch Dutch oven with 3–4 cups of water. I put that on a lot of coals as well. I put the lid on and let it simmer and cook, adding coals all the while to keep it hot. Also, since the beans continued to absorb water, I checked them from time to time. They will cook all by themselves.

While that was going on, I got the tomatillos chopped and added them into the 12-inch oven as well, with the chicken stock (which was stock that I made myself another day). Once the tomatillos and the chicken stock were in with the onions and pork, I put on the lid, and the rest of the time it cooked with the lid on, with only bottom heat.

Next, I sliced up the Anaheim chilies and added them to the 12-inch, without deseeding them, like I usually do. That will allow them to carry more picante flavor. Anaheims are pretty mild, anyway. Then, I added one jalapeño, also sliced, also without seeding, and let that cook for about a half hour. While that was going on, I added all the herbs and spices in the next ingredient group. Much of the spices and herbs were added more by taste, not so much by measure, by the way.

Then, after about a half hour, it was about time to check the heat. Taste it to see if it is spicy enough. If so, great—just let it keep cookin'. If not, then add another half jalapeño and let it cook for another half hour. I kept going like that until it was just as spicy as I liked it. Also, check the thickness. If it's too runny, whisk a tablespoon of flour in a half cup of water and pour a bit into the soup. Stir it up and let it thicken.

Once it was spicy enough, I let it simmer for another half hour or so.

I set up my little 8-inch oven with the rice and some water, and put that on some coals to boil. This was also done with the lid on and with only bottom heat. Once steam was venting from under the lid, I marked the time. About 10 minutes later, I took it off the coals and let it sit for another 15 minutes, still covered. I kept checking on the beans too, and by that time, they were done right (with a bit of salt) and ready to go. Dinner was served!

When I eat Chile Verde, I like to mix in the rice and the beans, tear up a flour tortilla, and scoop up the mixture in the tortilla. I don't know if it's more or less authentic; I just like the taste of all the foods mixed in. The rice adds undertone and texture, the pork and the chile give great savory and piquant flavor, especially with the lemon juice, and the tortilla has a bit of a salty zing to it.

# NUEVO MEXICAN DINNER

Out here in Utah are several chains of restaurants that do a kind of Mexican/southwest/fusion/modern-sorta semi-fast food. They're really popular. It started off with one, and a few copycat chains have sprouted as well.

This recipe is basically a copycat of their pulled pork burrito, but, as usual, I can't quite leave well enough alone! So I tweaked it to my own style. I guess it's not authentic to the restaurant, but then, it's not exactly authentic Mexican anyway!

It's basically three parts: pulled pork, beans, and rice, all tucked into a flour tortilla and folded up, with some sauces you can pour on top. I really like it, and my version, while not exactly like the restaurant, was still a really big hit with the family.

I cooked this in pretty large quantities for all of my wife's family on our recent travels. We had all gathered up at Bear Lake in northern Utah to celebrate the Fourth of July, and so I cooked this for all of them. I basically doubled the recipe below.

## PULLED PORK

### TOOLS

12-inch deep Dutch oven
12–15 coals below, and the same above

### INGREDIENTS

2 lbs. pork
1 (12-oz.) can regular (non-diet) cola
¼ cup brown sugar

salt
pepper
chili powder
garlic salt

1 (4-oz.) can diced green chilies
1 cup brown sugar
1 (14-oz.) can red enchilada sauce
1 (12-oz.) can regular cola

**FIRST I** prepared the pork. This was pretty straightforward. I put the meat in a zip-top back with the cola and brown sugar and let it sit for a long time. Were I to do this again, with better preparation, I would let it sit in a fridge overnight.

When the time came to cook the meat, I started up the coals. I planned on a standard heat, but I wanted to cook it a long time, to make it pull apart easier. I discarded the marinade and put the meat in to roast, with the seasonings. After about an hour or so, I added the canned ingredients. While it was cooking, I was a little bit worried about there being too much liquid. I had originally thought it would be like a roast, but it really turned into a braise. It turned out to be just right, after the pork was shredded.

After 2½–3 hours, the pork was pretty much ready to fall apart. I pulled it off the coals but left it in the Dutch oven. I grabbed a couple of forks and pulled the pork apart, stirring the braising sauces in as it shredded. Mine was boneless, but if yours isn't, remember to remove the bones!

I checked it frequently for quality control, of course. It was *muy* yummy!

In the final hour of cooking the meat, I also cooked the beans and the rice.

## BLACK BEANS

### TOOLS

12-inch shallow Dutch oven
18–20 coals below

### INGREDIENTS

3 Tbsp. olive oil
1 large onion, diced
1 large bell pepper, diced
3–4 cloves minced garlic
salt

3 (15-oz.) cans black beans, drained
salt
pepper
1–2 cups tomato juice
lemon juice
chili powder
cumin

chopped fresh cilantro

**I STARTED** by sautéing the first set of ingredients in the Dutch oven. As always, when sautéing, make sure that the pan and the oil are plenty hot before adding the ingredients.

The next set of ingredients went in, and I let everything cook together for a while. The beans in the can are already soft, so they basically just need to simmer with the other ingredients so all the flavors develop. Let it simmer until all of the other parts of the meal are ready. The longer it simmers, the better the flavors will blend. Finally, just as the dish was ready to serve, I stirred in the cilantro.

While the beans were cooking, I also made the rice.

## RICE

### TOOLS

10-inch Dutch oven
12–15 coals below

### INGREDIENTS

1 part rice, 1 part chicken stock (maybe more), 1 part water (maybe less)
1 tsp. butter
salt
3–4 garlic cloves, minced
juice of 1–2 limes
2 tsp. sugar
½ bunch of fresh cilantro, chopped (stirred in before serving)

flour tortillas

**I KNOW** these measurements are a little imprecise, but they work. I don't recall exactly how much I used, but I think there were 2 cups of rice and a total of 4 cups of liquid. The rest is just flavoring to taste.

When I make rice, I put in all the ingredients and then put it on the coals. I watch it until steam starts venting out from under the lid, and I let it cook for 5–10 minutes more. Then I remove it from the coals and let it sit, covered, for 10–15 minutes, to cook more and absorb more of the boiling water. I don't remove the lid (if I can help it) at all during the process. Usually, if I follow this procedure, the rice will be done very nicely, ready to fluff and serve!

The Dutch ovens themselves make great serving dishes, as each family member filed past. Start with a flour tortilla and add the rice and beans. Then, layer on the pulled pork and roll it up!

It was filling, and there was a lot left over! A great time!

# Central and South American

## ESCABECHE AND RICE AND BEANS

Back in the early '80s, I spent some time working for my church (an LDS mission) in Central America. That time included a six-month stay in Orange Walk Town in the northern parts of Belize.

Belize is a wonderful country with a small, tight-knit, yet diverse population. There are a lot of Hispanic people there, many from Guatemala, there are a lot of Caribbean Creole people there, and there are a lot of British there (because Belize used to be British Honduras). To that mix add Chinese and Hindu, and all in a town smaller than Paris, Idaho (trust me—that's small).

I learned a lot from teaching and working with these wonderful people. One of the things I learned was that you could make incredibly delicious meals without fancy pots or pans or even stoves. I remember meeting a guy outside his house one day. We all struck up a conversation. He had cut a big fifty-five-gallon oil drum off at about a third high and had a metal plate over it like a lid. He had it on top of hot coals and was shoveling more hot coals on top. What was he making? His wife had made coconut bread, and he was in charge of baking it (under her watchful eye). He told us to come back in about a half hour.

We did, and it was some of the most delicious bread I'd ever tasted.

One of the Church members there used to have us over for lunch a lot. He worked a hard day at the sugar factory, then he would come home and fix shoes for extra money. He took some of my worn-out, fancy Mr. Mac shoes and re-soled them with tire treads. That lasted me through the rest of the mission!

Anyway, his wife (and just about everyone else there in OWT) used to make this delicious onion, chicken, and vinegar soup, called "escabeche." Man, that was good stuff. It's really a staple of Belizean cooking. She had this little stand in the back of her house (a shack, really). She'd start a fire with wood chips and twigs and cook up the meal.

Two things stand out in my memory as defining Belizean cooking. One was this soup, and the other was their rice-and-beans dish. Both were humble "peasant dishes," if you will, but they were the most delicious things I'd ever eaten up to that point. And I made our branch president's wife teach me how to make it one day.

I've made it several times in the intervening years, and I finally made it in my Dutch oven. And, to complete the feast, I made the rice and beans.

A note about authenticity: I have made a few alterations to these recipes. But not much. Really, simplicity is good in these ones. Also, it goes to show that you don't have to have a snazzy professional oven to cook a great meal. Remember? Heat on food is all it's about!

Another note: As I've been traveling and interacting with people of different Latin backgrounds, I've discovered about three or four unique dishes, all bearing the name "escabeche." A few of them, notably the Peruvian one, are fish dishes. There are others, though. It seems that in most cases, the only thing they really have in common is the name.

So, if this doesn't look like your idea of what an "escabeche" recipe should look like, sorry. It *is* a Belizean escabeche, though.

## THE ESCABECHE

### TOOLS

12-inch Dutch oven
20+ coals below

10-inch Dutch oven
17+ coals below

### INGREDIENTS

2–3 lbs. chicken (I like the legs and thighs, but use what you like)
6 cups water

4–5 large white or yellow onions
¼ cup fresh chopped cilantro
½ tsp. thyme
liberal shakes of oregano
liberal shakes of salt and black pepper
liberal shakes of celery salt
2 Tbsp. minced garlic
1–2 jalapeño peppers, sliced

oil
½ cup lemon juice
2–3 cups white vinegar

corn tortillas

**I LIT** up some coals and started out with the chicken and the water in the 12-inch. It's simple enough: boil the chicken, with the Dutch oven covered.

While that was boiling, I sliced up the onions. You really need lots of onions. Slice up what you think is enough for a typical onion soup, and you're at about half what you'll need. Then add some more after that. This soup is mostly onion with some broth. Then, I added all the spices together in a bowl with the sliced onions and set that aside.

Once the 12-inch Dutch oven was boiling, I put the 10-inch Dutch oven on some coals, with a thin puddle of oil in the bottom. When the 10-inch oven was heated, it was just about the time that the boiling chicken was "done."

I pulled the chicken out of the broth, dripped it off, and set it to fry in the 10-inch Dutch oven in the oil. Be careful, because it'll splatter! I stirred and turned the chicken pieces to brown on all sides. That helps it get a little crunch and gives it a bit of fried flavor.

In the meantime, while the chicken was frying, I poured all the onion mixture into the broth in the 12-inch Dutch oven. I added the lemon juice and the vinegar. I always wonder how much vinegar to add. Generally speaking, I say go large and put in more toward the 3 cups. It depends on how daring your audience is. Still, without a good strong vinegar taste, this dish can end up wimpy. The lemon juice is my own addition to the recipe, and I really like the flavor it adds.

Then I added the browned chicken back into the onion and vinegar broth.

Normally, I'd say reduce the coals to just a simmer at this point, but since I was cooking in the dead of winter, I kept some strong coals on. Just let this cook until the onions are soft and the chicken has absorbed the vinegar.

While this was simmering, I worked on the rice and beans.

## THE BELIZEAN RICE AND BEANS

### TOOLS

10-inch Dutch oven
7 coals below
13 coals above

### INGREDIENTS

slices of salt meat (bacon, sausage, whatever ya got)
2 (15-oz.) cans red beans, with liquid
2 cups white rice
1 tsp. thyme

1 Tbsp. minced garlic
liberal shakes of salt and black pepper
½ cup coconut milk (about half a can)
¾ cup water

**AFTER FRYING** the chicken, I used the same hot 10-inch Dutch oven and coals to cook the salt meat. Usually, I use smoked sausage, sliced thin. Once that was browned, I added everything else, adjusted the coals as written, and cooked it, covered. I stirred it occasionally, until the rice was done.

Actually, you don't even need the meat. In most cases, Belizeans don't include it. But they sometimes do. I like it, myself. One lady used to make us rice and beans, and she serve it piled up high on the plate with a couple of pieces of barbecue chicken on top. *That* was yummy!

The two dishes were served side by side, the escabeche in a bowl, with corn tortillas on the side and the rice and beans on a small plate. The people in Belize often eat the escabeche without utensils, using pieces of the tortillas to pick up the onions and the chicken with their fingers. Some will fold the tortillas to make spoons to get the vinegar broth. Others just drink that from the bowl. We used to joke that a greenie missionary became a true Belizean elder when he could eat a whole heaping bowl of escabeche without touching his fork or spoon.

## JERK CHICKEN WITH SEASONED BAKED POTATOES

One night, I tried an experiment. I wasn't sure if it worked at the time. The end result was delicious, but I didn't really know if that was because of the technique I tried or in spite of it. In the years that followed, I've used this "dry roasting" technique a number of times, and now I know that it works!

I saw this recipe for jerk chicken, and it was really intriguing. But it's supposed to be grilled or broiled. That means that the marinade dries in place in a sort of glaze. Since Dutch ovens trap the moisture, that wouldn't happen. I thought to myself, what if I raised the lid a bit and let the moisture out. So I lifted the lid on a couple of sticks across the top. In subsequent attempts, I've tried different things. What I've finally settled on is three small U-shapes of heavy-gauge wire. These can be hooked on the rim of the Dutch oven and the lid set back down on them. There is room for the steam to vent, but it's not so open that it doesn't retain some heat. Still, I've found that I've had to put a lot of extra coals on the lid to make up for it.

I've also learned over time to bake it with a closed lid, as normal, and then change it up in the last 15–30 minutes. If there is still a lot of liquid in the Dutch oven at that point, I take off the lid and put a bunch of coals on the bottom to reduce out all the liquid in the Dutch oven, leaving only the sauce.

Anyway, here's the recipe.

## THE CHICKEN

### TOOLS
10-inch Dutch oven
6–7 coals below
12–14 coals above

### INGREDIENTS
3 Tbsp. lime juice
2 Tbsp. sweet juice (I used pineapple)
2 Tbsp. oil
1 tsp. soy sauce
5–6 stalks of green onions, chopped
1–2 jalapeños, cored, seeded, and chopped
2 Tbsp. allspice
½ tsp. cinnamon
shake of nutmeg
2 tsp. thyme
salt
black pepper

2 lbs. chicken (I used chicken tenderloins, but I'd also recommend boneless breasts)

**I STARTED** by mixing all of the first set of ingredients in a bowl. I put those all in a zip-top bag and added the thawed and dried chicken. I shook it all up to get it good and coated and put it in the fridge to marinate.

In the meantime, I started the coals and began working on the potatoes.

## THE SEASONED BAKED POTATOES

### TOOLS
12-inch Dutch oven
10 coals below
19–20 coals above

**INGREDIENTS**
5–6 medium potatoes
oil
sea salt
pepper
garlic powder
dried parsley

**I STARTED** by putting about a quarter inch of oil in the bottom of a bowl. I coated a potato in oil and then sprinkled it with the sea salt on all sides. I put that in the Dutch oven, then repeated that with all the others. Then I sprinkled the pepper, garlic, and parsley over all the potatoes. Those went on the coals for about 45 minutes, or until the potatoes were soft.

At that point, the chicken came out of the fridge, and I put it in the bottom of the 10-inch Dutch oven in a single layer. I put that on the coals and let it cook for 15–20 minutes. Then, I put the hooks on the rim of the lid and set the lid back on. I added an additional 8–10 fresh coals to the lid. I let that cook for 10–15 minutes, to set the glaze as much as possible.

When it's all done, serve it up with the potatoes!

## BRAZILLIAN-STYLE PARMESAN GARLIC BEEF CHUNKS

My wife and I went to a Brazilian barbecue house one day. I always love the exotic meats they make, and I love how they bring them by your table. Delicious stuff, and I want to learn how to make each one!

This time, one stood out for me. It was a delicious combination of garlic and Parmesan cheese. I had never tasted that on a chunk of steak before. I was enthralled. I wanted to figure it out, so every time the waiter brought it by I got, like, three chunks. I felt like a pig, but I had to get the tastes.

Then I had to adapt it to the Dutch oven because it's not being turned on a spit. I wasn't quite sure how to do that. At what point should I add the Parmesan and the garlic? As a sort of sauce at the end, or should I cook the steaks with it on?

These are the things that keep me up at night. Most definitely a first world problem . . .

## THE MEAT

### TOOLS

12-inch Dutch oven
20–22 coals below

### INGREDIENTS

2½ lbs. beef steak or roast
1 Tbsp. salt
1 Tbsp. pepper
½ Tbsp. paprika

## THE POTATO AND VEGGIE SIDE DISH

### TOOLS

10-inch Dutch oven
16–18 coals below

### INGREDIENTS

2–3 medium potatoes
1 medium onion
2 sweet peppers (of different colors)
olive oil
salt
pepper
parsley

## THE PARMESAN GARLIC DRIZZLE

### TOOLS

8-inch Dutch oven
10–12 coals below

### INGREDIENTS

3–4 cloves garlic
¼ cup butter
several very liberal shakes of Parmesan cheese

**SINCE I** had 3 Dutch ovens going to make this meal, I started a lot of coals. I cut the roast into 1–1½ inch squares. Think about a good kebab size. I seasoned the chunks by putting them in a zip-top baggie with the seasonings and shaking them up. I let them sit to absorb the flavors.

In the meantime, I started slicing up the veggies and potatoes for the side dish. Somewhere in all of this, I also spritzed the inside of the 10- and 12-inch Dutch ovens with a thin layer of oil and set them out on the coals to preheat. The 10-inch oven was for the veggie side dish, and the 12-inch was for the meat.

Then I added a drizzle of olive oil to each Dutch oven and let that heat to shimmering. I tossed the meat into the 12-inch oven and the veggies (with the salt, pepper, and parsley) into the 10-inch oven, and I gave both a stir to coat the food with the oil. I put a lid on the 10-inch oven and divided the coals evenly above and below, to bake the potatoes.

At that point, I had to pay close attention to the meat. I wanted to sear it and cook it medium or medium rare. Unfortunately, I found that my thermometers didn't work so well in such small pieces of meat. So, I just had to stir and guess. It didn't take long. I pulled them off the coals and put them on a plate under some aluminum foil to rest and settle.

In between all of that, I had minced up the garlic and added it, the butter, and the Parmesan cheese to the 8-inch Dutch oven. I put that on the coals, not so much to cook but to melt and blend.

Soon the potatoes were done, and it was time to assemble it all and serve it up. I put a few chunks of meat on each plate, brushed on the butter sauce (being very liberal with the cheese and the garlic chunks), and plated the veggies alongside.

It was amazing, and I dare say that I nailed the flavor to match the restaurant's version! I was amazed both by how elegant and exotic it looked and, at the same time, how simple the recipe was.

# AFRICA AND THE MIDDLE EAST

**AS REGIONS** and continents go, the ones that I've explored the least, in a culinary way, are Africa and the Middle East. This is kinda sad, actually, because there are many rich food traditions in these areas of the world—much of it native, much of it blended with the various foreign cuisines brought with the colonial era.

One tradition, brought to southern Africa by the Dutch, is the potjie ("poy-kee") pot. This is much like the Dutch ovens we use in America. It's cast iron and it has a lid and three legs to raise it up above the heat. This one, however, is rounded, like a bowl or a cauldron.

A stew, called "potjiekos," was made in the pot by travelers crossing the land with whatever meat and veggies they had on hand, or could hunt/gather as they traveled. It's interesting that the pot, once it's set on a low heat, is not stirred, keeping the flavors more separate. You'll read about this stew a little more in a bit.

On the other hand, one of the first meals I did in my new Dutch ovens was a traditional meat and potatoes dish from Palestine: Kofta bi Tahini

Here are some great dishes from this oft-overlooked continent!

# Northern African

## MOROCCAN LAMB TAGINE

Sometimes when I'm cooking, I get into ruts, and I get eager to try something new, something exotic. It happens a lot when the dishes I've been cooking have been remakes of past dishes. That's good—I mean, I get to learn how to do them again and make changes that make them better. But I also need to reach out and stretch from time to time too, or I get stale.

One week Jodi, my wife, had bought some lamb chops, and she was hoping that I'd do something with them. I dove in and searched out a whole bunch of lamb ideas from a whole bunch of cuisines and nationalities. In the end, this one won out, from Morocco.

This was my first attempt at anything from the African continent. Of course, it's from the northwest coast of Africa, and I'm well aware that central and southern cuisines are very different.

I also tried something new in my cooking process. Over the years, as I've been trying to learn how to cook, I've always kept a very loose and unorganized cooking space. This, of course, flies in the face of the concept of "mise en place." This is pronounced "miz-on-plas," and it means "everything in place." It's the act of gathering together all of your ingredients and utensils and arranging them into your working space so that you have easy access to them.

Up until this day, I'd never done this. I've only read about it.

But too many times I've run into situations where I've been in the middle of cooking a dish, and an ingredient I assumed we had plenty of was gone. Either it was misplaced, or it was used up or never there to begin with. In any case, I would usually be in a situation where the time for that ingredient came and went, and I was frantically searching for it, usually while other ingredients were burning.

As I looked over this extensive list of ingredients, especially the seasonings for the marinade, I realized that the time had come to embrace mise en place and give it a try. It really helped. Believe me. I have learned my lesson.

This recipe makes about six servings, at about 525 calories each. It was done in three steps: the marinade, the meat, and the stew.

## THE MARINADE

### INGREDIENTS

2 lbs. lamb meat
1 Tbsp. olive oil
2 tsp. paprika
¼ tsp. ground turmeric
½ tsp. ground cumin
¼ tsp. cayenne pepper
1 tsp. ground cinnamon
¼ tsp. ground cloves
½ tsp. ground cardamom
1 tsp. kosher salt
½ tsp. ground ginger
¾ tsp. garlic powder
¾ tsp. ground coriander

**AS I** mentioned, I began the night before by gathering up all of the seasonings and the meat so everything was there and accessible. I cubed up the lamb (from chops) and put it all in a 1-gallon zip-top baggie with the olive oil. I gave that a shake to coat the lamb.

Then I added in all of the seasonings. This is a serious whopping lot of seasonings. I followed the recipe, and it tasted great in the end, but I also wondered to myself if all of the individual flavors of all of these seasonings simply ended up lost in the mix. Maybe it's like a symphony orchestra. Sometimes it's the overall sound that's inspiring, not the individual instruments themselves.

Anyway, once all of those were in, I shook up the bag for about a minute, tossing the meat and massaging it so that all of it got well coated. I set it in the fridge to absorb overnight.

## THE MEAT

### TOOLS

12-inch Dutch oven
20–22 coals below

### INGREDIENTS

1 Tbsp. olive oil
the marinated meat from the previous step
2 medium onions, sliced
4–5 green onions, sliced into the green stems
3 cloves garlic, minced
1 Tbsp. fresh ginger, grated or minced
5 carrots, sliced lengthwise into thin, short strips

**EVEN THOUGH** the craziness of all the spices was done the night before, I decided to give mise en place another go the next day. I gathered up all of the ingredients before I did anything else.

I lit up the coals and then put the Dutch oven on with a bit of olive oil inside. I let that heat up a little. When I could tell that the oil was heated and shimmery, I dropped in the meat, and it began to brown. It looked sooooo good. The spices were browning and searing into the meat. Mmmm . . .

After about 10 minutes, I added in the onions, the garlic, the ginger, and the carrots. (I've been discovering the flavors of fresh ginger lately. It's cool.) I stirred that occasionally and cooked it until the onions became translucent.

## THE STEW

### TOOLS

20–22 coals below, a little less as it went on, to simmer

### INGREDIENTS

1 lemon, zested
juice of 1 lemon
2 cups chicken broth
2 Tbsp. tomato paste or sauce
1 Tbsp. honey

1 Tbsp. cornstarch (optional)
1 Tbsp. water (optional)
kosher salt to taste

**AFTER THE** onions became cooked a bit, I added the first set of stew ingredients. I covered it and let it come to a boil. I let a lot of the coals die out. I did replenish, but not as much as I might have for a roast, for example. Once it was boiling, I wanted it to simmer. I let it simmer for almost an hour.

When it was close to being done, I got out my 8-inch Dutch oven and made some rice.

Also, as it was nearing the end of the cooking time, I added the cornstarch (mixed with water so as not to clump) as a thickener. I also salted it a little more to bring out the flavors.

My family loved this international incident. My son helped himself to seconds without even asking. It was truly a success!

# Middle Eastern

## KOFTA BI TAHINI

My wife's cousin was married to a Palestinian man. He and I have become pretty good friends. He's pretty cool, but at first he had a tough time adjusting to life in America. Still, after a few years or so, he's catching on.

He makes a traditional Palestinian dish called kofta bi tahini. Kofta is a mixture of ground meat (usually beef, but sometimes lamb) and herbs and spices. It's shaped into a sort of cigar shape and then cooked in lots of different ways, like baking or grilling. But my favorite is when it's baked with potatoes and a tahini sauce.

My wife thinks this is kind of an acquired taste, but, personally, I acquired it fairly fast. I could chug this stuff nonstop. It does have a pretty strong taste. If you aren't used to foreign foods and you want to try this, then you could use a little less parsley and a little less lemon juice. But, to me, that's what makes it great.

Before I get into the process, there are a few special ingredients you need to acquire, and you might have to get them from a specialty store, possibly even a Middle Eastern market. If you can't find them, you can do some mixing (in some cases) and some substitutions.

One ingredient you really can't substitute is the tahini paste. It's like all-natural peanut butter, but it's made from ground sesame seeds. I can usually find it in health-food stores. It has a strong, nutty, and almost bitter edge, but when combined with the sour tones of the lemon juice it's just plain amazing.

Another necessary ingredient is a Middle Eastern blend of spices. You might have to get this from a Middle Eastern market. Sometimes it's just called "Middle Eastern spice" and sometimes it's called "baharat." If you can't find it, you can make it by following the blend I found online. There are lots of different blends of baharat. A good basic blend will include

- cumin
- cinnamon
- nutmeg
- turmeric
- coriander

If all else fails, you can just use allspice. It won't be the same, but it's still good.

A third issue is the meat. Most of the time I've eaten this it's been made of ground beef. This time, I tried it with ground lamb, and I think that made a big difference to the overall success of the dish. Of course, lamb is pretty expensive. In theory, you could use any ground meat, even turkey. No self-respecting Muslim would use pork, of course, but otherwise, go for it.

So, let's get started, shall we?

**TOOLS**
12-inch Dutch oven
10 coals below
16 coals above

**INGREDIENTS**
1 Tbsp. olive oil
1 medium onion, sliced
3–4 garlic cloves, minced
salt
2–3 medium potatoes, quartered and sliced, or sliced like big French fries

1 lb. ground meat (as mentioned, I used lamb this time)
1 Tbsp. baharat (or equivalent spices)
1 medium onion, diced
salt
pepper
⅓ cup fresh parsley, chopped
if you squeeze your lemon juice fresh (for the next set of ingredients), zest one of those lemons and add it here)

1 cup tahini paste
about ½ cup lemon juice
about ½ cup water

**I STARTED** by lighting up some coals, heating up the oil in the Dutch oven, and sautéing the onions and the garlic, with just a pinch or two of salt. Once those were browned and translucent, I added the potatoes. I stirred them to coat them with the oil and salt, and put the lid on. I didn't shift the coals to the top yet, though.

Next I made the meat mixture. It was pretty simple; I simply added all of the ingredients together and mixed them all up. Traditionally, the meat is formed into elongated meatballs, almost finger-shaped.

Then, I mixed up the tahini sauce. This was a little trickier. The amounts are estimates. I stirred in equal amounts of water and lemon juice, but only a bit at a time. You want two things to happen: the sauce needs to come to a thick, soup-like consistency, and there needs to be balance between the tastes of the lemon and the tahini. Words can't describe that balance, you just need to taste it along the way and see when it all blends right. I kept adding juice and water until it all looked and tasted right. A pinch of salt will also help bring out the flavors.

When everything was mixed, I opened the Dutch oven lid and arranged the meat sticks on top of the potatoes and onions. I poured the tahini sauce over it and then dashed in about ¼ cup more of water.

I adjusted the coals to the right amounts above and below for baking and set it to cook. It cooked for about 45 minutes. After about 30 minutes, the meat was getting cooked through, so I stirred it up. If you stir it up before that, it'll all break apart. When the potatoes are done, it's finished!

I also pulled out my 8-inch Dutch oven and cooked up some rice.

This dish is traditionally served with this Arabic salad (on the side):

- 2 cucumbers, chopped
- 4 small tomatoes, chopped
- ½ cup finely chopped parsley
- ½ jalapeño pepper, chopped
- small finely diced onion, chopped (optional)
- 1 tsp. salt
- ¼ cup lemon juice
- 1 Tbsp. olive oil (optional)
- ¾–1 cup of plain yogurt

Mix the cucumbers, tomatoes, parsley, jalapeño, and onion in a bowl. Just before serving, add the salt, lemon juice, and olive oil and stir. Last of all, spoon in the yogurt and stir it all up.

It was so much better this time than I'd ever made it before. I was in heaven. Even Jodi said it wasn't too bad when she came home.

I don't really know which one I like more, the kofta or the salad. I could chug them both down until I'm fit to explode.

# South African

## POTJIEKOS

As I mentioned before, in southern Africa there's a cooking tradition that utilizes cast-iron pots with rounded bellies and three cast legs to raise it up over the burning fire. They're called "potjie pots." The tradition has deep roots in South African history. They first learned to cook in cast iron from the Arabs to the north. In the colonial era, the Dutch settled South Africa and brought their own cast iron (the Dutch oven) with them.

The travelers who crossed the South African wilderness carried these pots with them, cooking up the wild game they hunted and the tubers and other vegetables they gathered along the way.

In modern day, the tradition of cooking in the pots continues, but it has evolved into an entire style, named "potjiekos." It literally translates to "potjie food" or "small pot food." This really isn't a dish so much as an approach to cooking. It's a big social event. A host will plan a party and invite friends over to socialize and celebrate while the food slowly cooks (which can take up to four hours, or even more in some cases).

The style I chose to emulate is a basic meat stew. It's created in three layers, and it's not stirred until it's completed and served. You start with meats as your bottom layer. These are usually braised for a long time to get them soft and tender. Then the next layer is made of veggies that are slower cooking. Finally, the top layer is the veggies that cook the most quickly. After reading some recipes, I could see which veggies to use in each layer. I also got ideas for spices.

In the end, I came up with my recipe, which was delicious. Not stirring was an interesting twist. It truly kept the flavors more distinct.

### TOOLS

12-inch deep Dutch oven
24+ coals underneath during browning
approximately 10–12 coals underneath during simmering

## INGREDIENTS

**The Meat**

½ lb. bacon
2–3 lbs. game meat (I got an elk roast)
1 cup flour
1 Tbsp. paprika
1 Tbsp. salt
1 Tbsp. pepper

**The Sauce**

1 (14-oz.) can beef stock
⅛ cup balsamic vinegar
1 (6-oz.) can tomato paste

**Slower-Cooking Veggies**

¼ of a 14-oz. can beef stock
2 medium sweet potatoes
4 large carrots
1 small sweet pumpkin
olive oil
salt
pepper
paprika
chili powder

**Faster-Cooking Veggies**

more beef stock, if necessary, from previous can
4 stalks celery
1 large onion
2–3 sweet peppers, of varying colors
4–5 cloves garlic
olive oil
salt
parsley
oregano

**I BEGAN** by heating up some coals and putting a lot of them under my 12-inch deep Dutch oven. I cut the bacon into small squares and put them on to sizzle. I let them cook, stirring occasionally, until they were very crisp.

While that was cooking, I cubed the game meat into chunks a little under 1 inch across. I mixed the flour and seasonings and tossed the meat chunks with them in a zip-top baggie. I pulled the meat out and shook off the excess powder.

Once the bacon was all fried up, I refreshed the coals a bit and tossed in the roast chunks. They started sizzling immediately. I did stir them, but only occasionally. I let them sear as much as I could before moving the pieces around. Soon, they had the look of being browned all around, and seared on a few sides. I let them cook about 20 minutes. The smell was incredible! A lot of crusty fond was also building up on the bottom of the Dutch oven. That would come in handy in a bit.

I didn't let the meat get done all the way through, but once it was mostly browned, I poured in a can of beef stock and added in the balsamic vinegar. The tomato paste could be added in now as well, but I did it much later, as it was an afterthought. I stirred it all up with a wooden spoon and scraped up as much of the fond as I could. I put the lid on it and let it come up to a boil.

The next part was both easy and tricky. It was easy because all I had to do was adjust the coals and keep it at a simmer for the next 2 hours. It was also tricky because I had to focus on maintaining the coals and keeping it at an even simmer for the next 2 hours. It wasn't hard or difficult work, but I had to watch the burning coals and the coals underneath, and I had to occasionally stir and check if it was simmering, boiling, or stagnant. For 2 hours.

By the way, the flour coating, in addition to helping brown and season the meat, also thickened the broth!

After 1½ hours, I peeled and chopped the sweet potatoes and the carrots, and I cored, seeded, and cubed up the pumpkin. Pumpkin is very common in African cuisine, I'm told. I coated them with a light dousing of olive oil and tossed them with the rest of the ingredients in that section. Go easy on the chili powder. It's there to give it some zing, not to make it a hot dish. Still, it's your dish, so do it as you like!

After one final stir of the meat, I poured on a layer of the slower-cooking veggies and evened it out. From that point on, until serving, I didn't stir the pot. I poured in about another quarter can of beef stock, around the edge so as to not rinse the seasonings off the veggies.

Then, I went back to napping—I mean, managing the heat under the pot! Yeah . . . That's it.

After a bit, I chopped up the celery, onion, and peppers, and I minced the garlic. I doused them with oil too and tossed them with their seasonings. About 45 minutes after I had put in the first batch of veggies, I added the last layer, along with about another quarter can of beef broth.

After a final round of cooking, another 45–60 minutes, I pronounced it done and brought it inside. It smelled heavenly! And after all these hours, I finally let myself stir up the food!

I served it up with some slices of bread that I also baked that day. It was delicious and filling! The flavors really were more distinct. I think not stirring the layers was a great idea. I also wasn't sure how I'd like the sweet potatoes and the pumpkin, but they were also delicious and added some sweet tones to an otherwise savory dish. The balsamic also brought some sweet along with the sour. The meat was moist and tender, and it fell apart. It didn't have any of the gamey bitter tones that so frequently come with elk or venison.

A delicious success!

# ASIA AND OCEANIA

**THE FLAVORS** of a culture's cuisine often evolve out of the foods that it has available natively. It amazes me when I realize that so many of the flavors we've come to expect as Americans and as part of Western European culture actually come from spices and herbs from the East, like ginger, nutmeg, cinnamon, even black pepper. None of those are native to our lands. In fact, much of the development of Western civilization has grown out of the results of the spice trade.

## Indian

### CHICKEN FEAST À LA INDIA

There are a lot of really good Indian restaurants where I live in the Salt Lake metro. I kinda assumed that other more "exotic" or more "cosmopolitan" cities have better restaurants. That might be true in some cases, but when I've been to other cities, I've noticed that the Indian food I've eaten there is about on par with the small, family-owned Indian restaurants here in Utah.

So, that brings me back to there being lots of really good Indian restaurants here in the Salt Lake metro.

And when I talk about "Indian," I'm talking, like, from India, not Native American. Just to clarify, because Salt Lake metro has some great Native

American food too. We're clear? Nobody's gonna turn me in to the PC Police?

When I eat Indian food, I always order two things: chicken tikka masala and chicken saag. Those are my all-time favorites. Sometimes, if I get a third thing, I might get tandoori chicken, or I might try something completely new that I haven't had before.

In my constant quest to find things I'm not supposed to be able to cook in a Dutch oven, I've now added these dishes. And since I love to combine them onto one rice plate, I had to try it. I dove in and did my research and found a number of recipes, which I basically followed.

I gotta tell ya, this is not for the faint-hearted, nor for the beginner. I ran like a madman from pot to pot, from one recipe to the other. I had to chart out in quarter-hour increments so that the saag, the tikka masala, and the rice would end up done at about the same time. This was *not* a relaxing meal to prepare.

Over time, I have streamlined the recipes a bit, combining some steps and adapting it so that I didn't have to run quite so much. Here's another warning: There are some unusual/exotic ingredients. You may have to go to an Asian/Indian market to find some of them, so you'll want to do some shopping first. Oh, but in the end it was worth all the extra effort!

### TOOLS

2 (12-inch) Dutch ovens
1 (10-inch) Dutch oven
lots of coals (20+), all underneath

### INGREDIENTS

**The Common Ingredients**
4 lbs. frozen chicken breast, thawed
olive oil
3 medium onions
3 Tbsp. minced garlic
2 inches fresh ginger
1½ cups rice
3 cups water

**For the Saag**
4 (16-oz.) bundles of fresh spinach
about ½ cup water
1 (14-oz.) can diced tomatoes
½ tsp. chili powder (cayenne, if you have it)
1 tsp. coriander

½ tsp. turmeric
1 tsp. cardamom
2 whole cloves
1 tsp. garam masala
4 Tbsp. milk
salt
pepper

**For the Tikka Masala**
1 (14-oz.) can tomato puree
4 Tbsp. plain yogurt
2 Tbsp. tikka masala curry paste
1 Tbsp. coriander
salt
pepper

**FIRST, GET** some coals on to burn. Lots. You'll need probably 3 beds of 20 or so each. We'll be cooking completely from the bottom, no coals on top, even though it will be cooked with all the pots covered. Make sure you have a side stack of burning coals as well so you can replenish.

Next, I cubed the thawed chicken. I put a little oil in the bottom of one of the 12-inch ovens and set that on the coals to brown. I chopped up the leaves of the spinach and put those in another 12-inch Dutch oven with about a half cup of water. I put that Dutch oven on coals to boil.

The Spinach will probably boil down long before the chicken is browned. I pulled the spinach out and drained it off, discarding the liquid. I mashed up the spinach so that it was almost a paste. I just kinda chopped at it with the point of a wooden spoon. When the chicken was browned, I pulled that oven off the coals as well and removed the chicken. I discarded any liquid in that Dutch oven too.

Next, I chopped up the onions, the garlic, and the ginger. I put them in one of the 12-inch Dutch ovens, put it back on the coals, and sautéed these ingredients until the onions were clear and a bit brown.

Here's where we split it up between the saag and the masala. I divided the onions and the chicken equally between the 12-inch Dutch ovens and put them both on the coals. I chose which oven was for the tikka masala and which was for the saag, and then I added all the respective ingredients and spices to each (the cooked-down spinach goes into the saag oven). I covered them both and let them cook, stirring occasionally. After they got boiling, I took some coals out from underneath so they simmered.

As the two dishes were cooking, I put the rice and the water into a 10-inch Dutch oven and put that, covered, on some more coals.

If you've timed it all right, then the rice, the chicken saag, and the chicken tikka masala will all be done at about the same time. It's not so critical if the chicken dishes cook a little longer, so whenever the rice is done, bring it all in.

To serve it, I put a bed of rice on the plate and covered half of it with the saag and half with the tikka masala. The two flavors complement each other, but I like them separate. When I eat it, I get a bite of one, with rice, and then the other.

Even my kids liked this one, though they did like the masala side more than the spinach on the saag side. Kids. Go figure . . .

## GARLIC NAAN AND PSEUDO-INDIAN CHICKEN

My wife's cousin was cleaning out her shelves in her house and had a whole bunch of books she was going to give to a thrift store. She offered me the chance to look through the box and pull any books I wanted before she took them away. I dug through and picked out an Asian cookbook.

So, we had her over for dinner, and I cooked some of those recipes.

My first thought was to do Indian because I found some things in there I'd been wanting to try. One of them was naan, and the other was tandoori chicken. But it turned out that we didn't have the right spices for the tandoori chicken, so I just followed the same procedure and recipe and used garam masala spices instead of tandoori masala. It definitely wasn't tandoori chicken, but it was good! I also used that "open oven" technique that I'd first tried with the Jerk Chicken (see page 117).

When I was making the naan, I saw that the measurement for the flour was in grams, and I needed to convert it to pounds. I, unfortunately, don't have a scale, so I just mixed it in until it felt nice and smooth and right.

So, as usual, the recipes below will reflect the way I actually did it, not so much what the book said.

## THE PSEUDO-INDIAN CHICKEN

### TOOLS
12-inch Dutch oven
10–12 coals below
20–24 (or more) coals above (depending on the outside temperature)

### INGREDIENTS
2–3 lbs. chicken (I used frozen chicken breast)
1 cup yogurt
4 Tbsp. garam masala powder
salt
oil

## THE GARLIC NAAN

### TOOLS
12-inch Dutch oven
10–12 coals below
20–24 (or more) coals above (depending on the outside temperature)

### INGREDIENTS
2 tsp. dry active yeast
4 Tbsp. warm milk
2 tsp. sugar

2–3 cups flour
1 tsp. baking powder
½ tsp. salt
⅔ cup milk
⅔ cup plain yogurt
1 egg
2 Tbsp. butter

½ stick soft butter
2 Tbsp. minced garlic
liberal shakes of parsley and thyme
salt and pepper

**SINCE I** cooked these things at the same time, I'll go over the instructions as I did them. There's a few suggestions I'll throw in that I hope to remember to do next time.

I patted the thawed chicken dry and cut a few slices into the chicken so the spices could more easily penetrate. I put it in a bowl with the yogurt, the garam masala powder, the salt, and the oil and stirred it up. I set this aside for a couple of hours.

Then, I mixed the first set of ingredients in the naan section to activate the yeast. I let it sit until it got frothy and then added the next set of ingredients. I mixed it all together (a little shy on the flour), then turned it out onto the floured tabletop to knead. As I kneaded it, I added more flour bit by bit until it felt right, smooth and satiny. Then I set aside the dough to rise.

When I came back a couple of hours later, the chicken and the bread were both almost ready.

I lit up a lot of coals. (Hey, it was cold out!) The tandoori chicken is normally cooked in a special oven that cooks with a very dry heat so the marinade gets baked onto the chicken dry. Dutch ovens, of course, trap the steam and hot moisture under a heavy cast-iron lid. Also, if you just put the chicken in the bottom of the oven, the juices will gather around the chicken. My solution was to put the chicken in one of those folding steamers (so the juices would drip down below) and put that into the Dutch oven. I dealt with the lid another way (see method below). I put that oven on the coals to begin cooking.

I oiled the other 12-inch Dutch oven up and put it on and under the coals to preheat.

Then, I cut the dough into quarters and rolled and spread each quarter until flat on the floured tabletop. I had mixed the butter and the spices, so I spread that over each flat. I put one flat into the Dutch oven. After 3–5 minutes, I opened up the lid and turned the bread over to cook for another 3–5 minutes. Then I pulled it out and put in the next one.

In the meantime, the chicken was cooking. I put some more of the sauce/marinade on after a bit. After about 20 minutes on the heat, I figured the chicken was about half done. I had this set of tongs that I balanced across the rim of the Dutch oven and put the lid back on it. That lifted the lid enough to let the steam vent, but not so much that too much heat was lost as well. Another idea I had was to get a few 2-inch nails, at least 3 of them, and to bend them into a U-shape. Place them over the side of the Dutch oven so when the lid is put back on, it sits high. I put a lot of extra coals on the lid so there was extra heat radiating from the top as well.

The yogurt and spice marinade cooked onto the chicken as a sort of glazed coating. It was really delicious.

After about another 20 minutes, the chicken was done and ready. In the meantime, I'd also made some rice with lemon juice to serve on the side.

There are many ways to serve this. One is to put the chicken on a bed of rice and put the naan on the side. Another is to put the rice and chicken onto the naan and then fold it over to eat it. Try it how you like it! This might not have been authentic tandoori chicken, but man, it was goooood!

# East Asian

## MASSAMAN CURRY

Just like Indian restaurants, there are many little mom-and-pop Thai restaurants in northern Utah. I've been to a lot of them, and most of those are really good. In fact, while I've liked one or two more than the others, there isn't one that I'd consider to be "bad" at all. I really like Thai food, and one of our favorite dishes to order is massaman curry.

If you have certain ingredients, it's actually pretty simple to make. The toughest ingredients to get are the tamarind pulp and the curry paste. And those really aren't that hard. I found some dried tamarind pods at a Mexican market, and I had to extract the pulp. The pulp is the sticky, pasty stuff that's around the seeds in the pods after you shell them. It's really nasty to work with. I separated the seeds, put in a little water, and microwaved it until it boiled. Wait—did I use a microwave? Yes, I did. . . . Then I stirred it all pretty vigorously to help it dissolve away from the seeds and pulled the seeds out, leaving the pulp. Since that first experience, I've also done it by simply boiling the seeds and the water in the 8-inch Dutch oven.

The Mexicans make a juice out of it that's really, really good. I guess in Thai and Indian food, it's used more as a flavoring.

This curry didn't end up being very spicy. Not spicy at all, in fact. I think it was a really mild curry paste that I used. But I've had massaman that's scorching. I like it best as a medium zing. This one was nice because it was flavorful even if it wasn't overly hot 'n spicy.

**TOOLS**
12-inch Dutch oven
about 20 coals below

**INGREDIENTS**

1–2 Tbsp olive oil
2 Tbsp. curry seasoning (I bought it out of a box, not the little bottles of "curry powder")
4 cloves garlic, minced
3 medium onions

2 (14-oz.) cans coconut milk
½ cup peanut butter

6–7 medium potatoes
1–2 lbs. meat (this time I used about equal portions of cubed chicken and uncooked peeled shrimp)

up to 1–1½ cups water
½ tsp. ground cardamom
4 bay leaves
3 Tbsp. sugar
3 Tbsp. tamarind pulp, or some splashes of tamarind juice/nectar
½ cup chopped unsalted peanuts
¼ cup chopped coconut
3 tsp. salt
liberal shakes of cinnamon

**FIRST, I** got the Dutch oven onto the coals (the entire dish was done with bottom heat), and put the oil in the bottom. After it had heated, I added the curry seasoning. I mixed that in the oil and let it activate in the heat a little before I added the garlic and the onions to sauté. If you wanted, you could add some chopped green pepper and/or celery here. Maybe some green onions.

Once all that was nicely sautéed and translucent, I added the coconut milk and the peanut butter. You could add the peanut butter by the spoonful; then it would be in smaller chunks and dissolve a little better.

I chopped up the potatoes and cubed the chicken and added those to the heating coconut milk. I also added in the shrimp. Once I put the meat in, I covered it with the Dutch oven lid to help it trap the heat.

I let the liquid get warm again and added in the remaining ingredients. I let these simmer, covered, for about an hour or so on the coals, while I made the rice. The water listed is primarily to help adjust the overall liquid level. You could also dust in a little cornstarch or flour to thicken it up, if need be, right at the end of the cooking. Also, taste it while it's simmering to see if the spices are hot enough for your taste. If not, add a little chili powder or more curry dust, let it simmer, and then check it again.

I served it over rice, and it was delicious! For me, I love the peanut and coconut richness, adding sweet tones to the savory of the meats and spices. If it's got some good, strong piquance too, then that's even better!

## MONGOLIAN STIR-FRY

Have you noticed a trend in this book? I get most of my ideas for international dishes by eating out.

There are some local Chinese restaurants here in Salt Lake City that do something called "Mongolian stir-fry" (sometimes "Mongolian barbecue"). You get a bowl and you go through this line like a buffet. First you pass the meats, which are sliced really thin, almost like potato chips. Then you go past noodles and vegetables. You get to choose what you want, and you put it all in your bowl. Then you get to pour in all kinds of sauces and add garlic and hot sauce if you like.

Then you hand it off to a chef, and he or she puts your food on this big round metal disc like a table, heated with gas from below. The chef flips it and tosses it. If you're lucky, you get a chef who's a bit showy about it. Finally, in a whoosh, they scrape the cooked food off the cooking table and onto your plate and hand it to you, ready to eat.

I love it. It's great food, and it's fun to watch. One thing I love about it is, like wok stir-fry, the veggies are cooked but still crisp.

Like I always do when I taste great food in a restaurant, I got to thinking that I could do that in my Dutch oven. So, of course, I tried it. This is actually a lot of fun for entertaining. All of the family members and guests can choose what they want on their own plate.

### TOOLS

8-inch Dutch oven
8–10 coals each above and below

12-inch Dutch oven
20+ coals below

### INGREDIENTS

1 cup rice
salt
2 cups chicken broth

olive oil

**The Mongolian Stir-Fry Line**
chicken, sliced thin
beef, sliced thin
pork, sliced thin
shrimp
mushrooms, sliced
celery, sliced
onions, sliced
bean sprouts
snow peas
and any other veggie you care to add

**The Sauces/Seasonings**
minced garlic
soy sauce
vinegar
teriyaki sauce
hot sauce
salt
pepper
other herbs and spices
any other oriental market sauces you care to add

**I STARTED** out by lighting and heating up the coals for the 8-inch Dutch oven. Light extras, because you'll be using more for the 12-inch, and you'll need them to keep the fires going. While those were getting hot and white, I sliced up the meat and the veggies.

I put the rice, the salt, and the broth into the small Dutch oven and put it on the coals. The way I cook rice is to simply watch it for steam venting. That tells me that it's been boiling for a bit at that point, and I just keep it on for about another 10 minutes. Then I pull the coals off and just let it sit for a while longer with the lid on. The less you remove the lid, the better. If you can cook it completely without ever lifting the lid, you've perfected the art of cooking rice in a Dutch oven!

Once the rice was on the coals, I set up the side fire with more coals. By the time the rice was almost done, those coals were ready. I put those coals on my little Dutch oven table and put the 12-inch Dutch oven on them, no lid, with a couple shakes of olive oil on the bottom. Then I called the family to dinner!

They picked up bowls in the kitchen and filled them with the ingredients they wanted, including the sauces and spices. They brought these to me, the chef!

By this time, the Dutch oven and the oil was heated, and I took the first bowl and poured it in. I had a couple of wooden spoons and I used them to stir the food as it was cooking. At first, I just did a quick stir to make sure it all got coated with the oil, then kept it cooking, stirring and tossing it every few minutes.

While that was cooking, I put rice in the bottom of each guest's bowl, and when the stir-fry was all done (I might have added a little salt, pepper, and garlic occasionally), I scooped it out with the spoons and put it onto the rice. Maybe 3–5 minutes tops, dinner *done*!

This would be a great way to host a party. You'd just have to make sure that you had enough ingredients and rice for everyone. You could even have 2–3 Dutch ovens going, each cooking the stir-fry.

## SUSHI

Sushi? In a Dutch oven?

Well, Mark, you have finally lost it. You've gone too far. Now we're going to have to call the Dutch Oven Police on you. Sushi? Really? That can't be legal . . .

Okay, okay, technically, I only made the rice in my Dutch oven. That's really all you cook, anyway, right? But still, can you imagine making such an exotic meal out in the woods somewhere? It's a cool thought!

Brendon and I have made sushi seven or eight times now, indoors. I admit that, with that little bit of experience, we're hardly expert chefs. But we have been able to make it work pretty well and have created some good and simple rolls. Let me share with you what I've learned.

One thing I love about sushi is that the flavors are so understated. Some things I eat, like a good barbecue or Mexican dish, are filled with bold, strong, spicy flavors. Sushi is filled with subtlety and complexity. Even the undertone of the rice and the nori are layered with the sweet and sour of the sugared vinegar. The unseasoned fillings combine their natural sweet tones and delicacy. It's no wonder that people spend their entire lives trying to be great sushi chefs.

### THE RICE

#### TOOLS

10-inch Dutch oven
about 18 coals underneath

8-inch Dutch oven
about 10 coals underneath

a wide wooden spoon or spatula
a handheld fan, or something that works like it
a nonmetallic bowl, preferably wooden, preferably wide and shallow

**INGREDIENTS**
3 cups Japanese short-grain rice
3¼ cups water (for cooking, not including water for rinsing)
⅓ cup rice vinegar
3 Tbsp. sugar
1 tsp. salt

**ONE THING** I've learned is that, like many other dishes, the process of making rice is as important as the ingredients, beginning even before I start cooking. I took three cups of Japanese short-grain rice and put it in a bowl. I filled it with water until the rice was well submerged, and I stirred it and turned it with my hands. Instantly, the water became a murky white. After a few turns with my hand, it seemed it wasn't getting any cloudier, so I carefully drained as much as I could without spilling the rice into the sink. Then I filled it back up with fresh water and swished and rinsed it again. And again. And again.

I've never gotten to the point where the water flowed completely clear, but I have been able to rinse it so that it was almost clear, or at least significantly clearer. I usually do it at least 6 or 7 times.

Finally, I put the rice in a strainer and let it sit over my sink for about a half hour. That's when it's ready to cook. While the rice was straining, I lit up my coals and let them get hot.

I put the rice and the water into my 10-inch Dutch oven, and set that on the coals with the lid on. I let it sit there for 20–25 minutes. Normally when I cook rice, I watch for venting steam, but this time I didn't see any, so I had to carefully watch the clock. Keep in mind that the Dutch oven has to heat up too. I didn't lift the lid at all.

Once the rice time was done, I pulled it off the coals and set it aside. I didn't lift the lid. It sat for quite some time, easily another 20 minutes.

While that was finishing the final stages of cooking, I mixed the rice vinegar, the sugar, and the salt in the 8-inch and put that over some coals, uncovered. I stirred that and let it dissolve to a low, rolling boil. Then I pulled it off and let it cool some.

Combining the rice and the vinegar is an odd process. I dumped the rice into the nonmetallic bowl. While slowly stirring the rice with the spoon or spatula, I would alternately use my other hand to pour in some of the vinegar mix and fan away the moisture and steam. Stir, pour, fan, stir, pour, fan. Sometimes when Brendon and I do this together, one of us fans while the other pours and stirs. If you're using one of the traditional shallow wooden bowls, the wood will also help wick away some of the moisture in the rice.

When it was all done, I was left with well-cooked rice, clinging to itself in clumps, with individual grains still visible (not a paste). It had a delicious sweet-and-sour taste. This got set aside to get closer to room temperature.

With the rice all ready and cooling, it was time to prepare the filling ingredients. Here is a list of all the ingredients we usually gather to make our various sushi rolls:

## THE SUSHI

### TOOLS

a sushi rolling mat
a large cutting board
a sharp knife
a bowl of water
a damp towel

### INGREDIENTS

6–8 sheets of nori (roasted seaweed)
the sushi rice
1 thick, small fillet of salmon, uncooked
1 thick, small tuna steak, uncooked
crab leg meat, cooked
1 cucumber
1–2 carrots
1–2 avocados, sliced
white and black sesame seeds
1 (8-oz.) package cream cheese

**For Serving**
soy sauce
wasabi paste
pickled ginger slices

**THE MEATS** need a little bit of preparation. If the fish was frozen, it should be completely thawed and patted dry with paper towels. I cut the skin away from the salmon. We usually use imitation crab. I know I should hang my head in shame, but at least we can afford it.

I peeled the cucumber and quartered it lengthwise. I scooped out the seeds with a spoon and sliced it lengthwise into very thin strips. I cut the carrots into long, thin strips as well.

I arranged everything in the list of ingredients and tools around my cutting board so I could reach whatever I wanted to put into any particular roll. Mise en place, remember? Finally, it was time to make sushi!

I placed the rolling mat on the cutting board in front of me, arranged so I would be rolling away from myself. I put a sheet of nori, shiny side down, onto the rolling mat. Then I got my hands good and wet in the bowl and grabbed a palmful of rice. I spread that out over the nori. There's an art to spreading the rice, which I have not yet learned. The trick is to spread it thinly and gently, without smashing the grains of rice. You should be able to see spots of nori through the clumps of rice.

I've read about and watched lots of techniques. I used a whole sheet of nori and I spread enough rice to cover all but about ¾ of an inch at the far edge. Some use half sheets. You can play with it and see.

Once the rice was spread, I laid my filling ingredients in a horizontal line, about an inch from the near edge of the nori. I started by slicing off a thin bit or two of tuna or salmon and laying that down. I put on any other ingredients I wanted, such as the cucumber, the carrots, or the avocado. You can sprinkle the sesame seeds in at this point, but I like to sprinkle it over the sliced pieces when I'm done. I sliced the cream cheese off with a regular butter knife and laid it onto the roll in strips.

I had to resist the urge to put too much in a roll. I love to just keep putting stuff in, but I know that it muddies up the tastes and makes it harder to roll.

If you or any of your guests don't like the idea of eating raw fish, use the crab. I've even cooked the fish and put it in the sushi before, but I don't like it as much myself.

Once I'd laid in my fillings, I curled up the near end of the rolling mat, with the nori, and curled it up and over the ingredients. I'll often use my fingers to hold the ingredients in place as I'm doing the curl. I rolled it over and pulled the leading edge of the mat away as it rolled the nori underneath. I squeezed as I rolled, but I had to be cautious not to squeeze too much, so as to keep the rice from smooshing.

The last bit of nori, where there's no rice on the end, got a little bit of water from my fingers to help it seal. Then, with a couple of squeezes, the last bit of rolling was complete. I pulled the mat away and picked up the knife. I wiped it with the damp cloth, and in a couple of quick motions, I cut the roll in half. I turned the two halves I'd cut to be side-by-side. I wiped the blade again and cut the slices of the roll together, two more times, to make a total of six pieces. I wiped the blade between each cut. Making sure that the blade is clean and damp will keep it from sticking when you cut.

Finally, each piece was set on the plate, with a dollop of wasabi paste and a few bits of the pickled ginger. Add a small bowl of soy sauce, and you're on your way!

Now, while it might not have been as good as I could get in a fine sushi bar in Tokyo, or even the more metropolitan areas of the states, it still tasted great, and I had a lot of fun making it too!

# Polynesian

## PULLED PORK AND PINEAPPLE

One weekend, Jodi gave me this recipe for a really simple pulled pork roast that turned out really good. The recipe was originally for a slow cooker, so I modified it a bit for the Dutch oven, but not too much. Truly, a Dutch oven was the original slow cooker!

### TOOLS

12-inch deep Dutch oven
12–14 coals above
10–12 coals below

### INGREDIENTS

4–6 lbs of pork roast (I had two loin roasts that I think were 2½–3 lbs. each)
liberal shakes of salt, pepper, thyme, parsley

1 (20-oz.) can pineapple chunks, with juice
1 jar apricot preserves
3 apricots, sliced thin
2 Tbsp. soy sauce
¼ cup mustard
more salt and pepper
liberal shakes of cinnamon
juice of 1 lemon

**I STARTED** by putting the spices in the first set on the roasts and rubbing them in a bit. Then I put them in the 12-inch deep Dutch oven and roasted them. I pretty much went with a "low and slow" approach to the heat. I kept the coals replenished, but always on the low side of the counts. I wanted it to take a longer time to cook, and just to take it easy. I actually roasted for about 3 hours.

When the thermometer said they were done, they looked really, really good just as they were. I thought about just slicing and serving them as is. But I pulled them out and shredded them with the fork. I put them back into the pot. After you stir it all back in, if there's too much liquid, you can remove some with a basting syringe or a spoon. Alternately, you can sprinkle in some flour or cornstarch to thicken it up a little.

I put the Dutch oven back out on the coals, but this time in more of a baking configuration, with more heat on top. I added all of the ingredients in the second set.

I cooked it a while longer, also low and slow, and allowed all the flavors to meld together. Finally, it was all done. You could serve it with potatoes or on rice. It's yummy!

# COMING BACK HOME

**SO, I** was trying to think of a way to wrap up the virtual culinary travels in this book in a nice, tidy package and put a ribbon on it. This book represents a lot of what I've been going through as I've learned how to cook in a Dutch oven. It's not just a journey through different continents and cuisines; it represents much of my own learning journey.

So, after some thought, I decided to bring it all back home with one more recipe. One that's about as nonexotic and nonexploratory as you can get. A good old American beef stew with biscuits. Comfort food. No surprises, no twists—just traditional, delicious, and filling!

## BEEF STEW WITH EVERYTHING

### TOOLS

12-inch Dutch oven
18–20 coals below

### INGREDIENTS

1–2 lbs. stew beef
salt and pepper

2 capfuls (or shakes) of olive oil, plus more
1 cup sliced mushrooms
2 sweet peppers, chopped (I like to choose a green one and one of a different color, like red or yellow—it adds color and a slightly different flavor)
2–3 celery stalks, sliced

1–2 medium onions, sliced
2 Tbsp. minced garlic

1 (14-oz.) can beef broth

2 medium to large potatoes, quartered and sliced
1 large carrot, sliced
2 medium tomatoes, chopped
1 jalapeño, seeded, cored, and sliced
½ Tbsp. crushed bay leaves (or crumble a few whole leaves)
1 Tbsp. parsley
½ Tbsp. thyme
liberal shakes (maybe ⅙ cup) of balsamic vinegar
salt
pepper

2 Tbsp. flour

**I STARTED** by lighting up about 25 or so coals. While those were heating up, I cut the stew beef up into ½- to 1-inch cubes and seasoned them with salt and pepper. I let them set for a bit. I also prepared the veggies in the second set of ingredients.

When the coals were heated, I put about 20 of them underneath my Dutch oven and put a little olive oil in the bottom. I let that heat up until the oil was shimmery. I wanted the oven to be really hot but not burning the oil. I tossed in the meat chunks and gave them a quick stir. I wanted these to have a good sear with a caramelized brown, so I didn't stir it much, but I occasionally tossed it. I also didn't want it to fully cook, just to sear.

After a few minutes, I pulled the meat out and let the oven heat up again with a little more olive oil. All of that delicious brown fond on the bottom of the pan helped flavor the stew!

I added some oil into the Dutch oven, and then I tossed in the aromatic veggies in the second set and let them sauté in the fond, with a little salt to draw out the moisture. I love the smell of that.

When the onions were looking clear and the mushrooms were starting to shrivel and brown, I added the meat back in and then the broth. I put the lid on because it boils easier that way. I added in the fourth set of ingredients, a few at a time, as I got them chopped and prepared. I added any extra broth or water as I thought it needed. I do like it to be more of a stew than a soup, though.

Within 15–20 minutes, it started boiling, so I removed a few coals (maybe 4 or so), to reduce the heat a little. I still had some coals going in my side fire, and I added some to it from the bag from time to time to be able to have hot ones to replenish the ones under the Dutch oven.

Every half hour or so, I opened up the Dutch oven and stirred the stew. Regulating the heat wasn't that tricky. As the coals died down, I added new ones from the side fire. The total cooking time was probably 1½–2 hours. My gauge was the potatoes. When they were done, I was safe, and I cooked it a bit longer just for more flavors.

At the end, I added the flour as a thickener. I imagine that I could have added it at the beginning, and it probably would have been okay, but I think it maintained the thickness better. I've heard that tapioca powder is a really good thickener, and it can be added at the beginning.

This is a really yummy, basic stew. I love to serve it with the biscuits below. You want a twist? When you serve this stew, garnish it with a few crumbles of feta cheese!

## THE BISCUITS

### TOOLS

12-inch Dutch oven
12–15 coals below
24–28 coals above

### INGREDIENTS

olive oil
2+ cups flour
½ tsp. baking soda
2 tsp. baking powder
2 Tbsp. shortening
1 cup buttermilk

**I STARTED** by lighting the coals and letting them get a bit white. When they were ready, I oiled the inside of my Dutch oven and set it, empty, on and under the coals. I wanted it to get good and hot!

While that was heating, I mixed the dry ingredients and then added the shortening, cutting it all together with a pastry knife. You can also blend it with your hand, but if you do that too much, you can warm it up, and it will poof better if the oils are cool.

Then I mixed in the buttermilk and continued cutting with the pastry knife. After it was well mixed, I kneaded it a bit, but not much. I only did a few folds, and then I rolled it out on the floured countertop. I rolled it to about a half inch thick.

Then, using a small child's drinking glass, I cut the circles and set them aside on a plate. The extra dough was wadded up, rerolled, and recut. Then I took the plate out to the hot Dutch oven and set the dough circles in the bottom. Sometimes I'll spread some melted butter on the tops. That makes them taste great and browns them better.

I put the lid back on and baked the biscuits for about 10–20 minutes.

Serving the biscuits alongside the beef stew makes for an absolutely delicious comfort meal. A wonderful thing to come home to after all the culinary travels and experimentation.

**I HOPE** you've enjoyed journeying with me. I've learned a lot along the way, and I hope you've learned a few things too. Come visit me at marksblackpot.com and tell me of your travels and experimentations!

# BONUS CHAPTER: EXPLORING FOOD

**ONE THING** I've loved about my cooking adventure has been the constant learning. There is *so* much to discover and *so* much to try. International cuisines have given me a lot of opportunities to explore and add to my culinary experiences. And just when I start to get comfortable and proud of myself, I discover some new tradition that I've never seen before, or I start to realize that I'm not as good at something as I thought I was, and, suddenly, I have something new to learn!

In addition, I like to give myself challenges to find new things and try things in new ways.

This bonus section is all about exploring food, learning, and discovering. All in that most traditional of cooking utensils: a Dutch oven! Oh, the irony!

## Cooking Challenges

### OVERVIEW

My son Brendon, a budding chef in his own right, absolutely loves to watch competitive cooking shows. I have mixed feelings about them myself. He loves to see the chefs running around like crazy, throwing odd foods together, chopping, boiling, stewing, freezing, frying, and plating until suddenly someone yells, "Chefs! Step back! Your time is up!" and they throw their hands in the air and step away from their tables.

What I don't really like about them is that they're more focused on the drama of the event than the cooking. I don't learn a lot about cooking and how ingredients work together from these shows. I admit that I do, occasionally, get an interesting idea to try. Still, mostly, it's about the competition, not the cooking.

One thing I do like about the shows, however, is that the chefs are intentionally forced out of their comfort zones. They are set up to compete in awkward or downright hostile environments, with a ridiculous time constraint, with ingredients that most of them had probably only heard of before. I do like that challenge. I do like stretching myself that way. I do like creating odd parameters and difficult situations where I am forced to invent and adapt. I like cooking challenges.

For me, cooking challenges evolved out of an online game that Andy (my good friend and author of backporchgourmet.com) and I have played off and on for the last few years. It all began when he threw down the cast iron gauntlet and told me to cook a meal with three seemingly random ingredients: a meat, a starch or veggie, and a spice or flavoring.

I did the dish and then responded with another challenge for him. All of this is chronicled in the final chapter of my first book, *The Best of the Black Pot*, where I talk about cooking without a recipe and making your own recipes. It was just like on the show, where we had to "open up our virtual ingredient basket" and cook something with what was there. After that first challenge, we had so much fun that we have continued back and forth to this day.

From there, our challenges grew. I began to explore other approaches and ways to randomize the ingredients, and I developed another strategy, called "Deconstruction." This will be explained a bit later in more detail, but really the basic idea is to take a familiar dish, mentally break it down into its core ingredients, and then create a new dish using those same ingredients.

Really, any circumstance where you have to cook and create within unusual parameters is a good challenge. The idea is to force you to think outside of your comfort zone beyond ingredients and cuisines that you're familiar with. You have to dig deeper to come up with ways to rearrange and rethink things you might or might not be familiar with.

## RANDOM INGREDIENTS

Way back in the day, when I was in high school and early college, I used to play all kinds of role-playing and adventure games. One aspect of those games is rolling dice and consulting tables to find out what happens next.

So, when I want to tackle something like a randomization of ingredients and parameters to challenge my cooking, I look to my gaming roots.

As a result, here's a version of our game that I've turned up to eleven. Here's how it works. The first table is the meat table. Roll an ordinary six-sided die (you know, like the ones in your old Yahtzee game). And look at the first column for your result. Next to it will be another column. Roll again, and that will be the meat ingredient you'll cook with. Here's the table:

| First Roll | Second Roll |
|---|---|
| 1 or 2: Red meat | 1: Beef |
| | 2: Lamb/mutton |
| | 3: Buffalo |
| | 4: Venison |
| | 5: Other game meats |
| | 6: Ostrich |
| 3 or 4: White meat | 1: Pork |
| | 2: Chicken |
| | 3: Turkey |
| | 4: Cornish hens |
| | 5: Duck |
| | 6: Other game bird |
| 5: Seafood | 1: Salmon |
| | 2: Trout or other game fish |
| | 3: Tuna |
| | 4: Crab |
| | 5: Shrimp or lobster |
| | 6: Other seafood |
| 6: Other meat | 1: Cold cuts |
| | 2: Sausage |
| | 3: Bacon or proscuitto |
| | 4: Dried meats |
| | 5: Nonmeat proteins |
| | 6: Other meat products |

So, let's say you roll the die, and it comes up as a 3. That would mean that you're on the "White Meat" section. Let's say that your next roll is a 4. That would mean that your first mystery ingredient would be . . . drum roll please . . . Cornish hens! Go out and buy some! By the rules of this game, you're allowed to use them in any form and cook them in any way.

Let's go on to the next table: the fruits, veggies, and grains.

| First Roll | Second Roll |
|---|---|
| 1 or 2: Starch | 1: Potatoes |
| | 2: Bread |
| | 3: Rice |
| | 4: Pasta |
| | 5: Corn |
| | 6: Other starch |
| 3 or 4: Vegetable | 1: Legumes, beans, peas |
| | 2: Aromatics (onions, celery, garlic) |
| | 3: Broccoli or cauliflower |
| | 4: Yellow squash or zucchini |
| | 5: Greens (spinach, collard, and so on) |
| | 6: Other vegetables |
| 5 or 6: Fruit | 1: Apples |
| | 2: Citrus |
| | 3: Tomatoes |
| | 4: Kiwi |
| | 5: Pineapple |
| | 6: Other fruits |

Here is the last of the ingredient tables—the spices and flavorings!

| First Roll | Second Roll |
|---|---|
| 1 or 2: Spices | 1: Paprika |
| | 2: Cinnamon |
| | 3: Cardamom |
| | 4: Fennel Seed |
| | 5: Cloves |
| | 6: Chili powder or other hot pepper |
| 3 or 4: Herbs | 1: Parsley |
| | 2: Cilantro |
| | 3: Sage |
| | 4: Thyme |
| | 5: Basil |
| | 6: Other herbs |
| 5 or 6: Other flavorings | 1: Lemon juice |
| | 2: Vinegar |
| | 3: Vanilla |
| | 4: Cocoa |
| | 5: Other drink |
| | 6: Other flavoring |

The following table needs a little explanation. These are things to throw in the mix to make it even more tricky, more challenging, more complex. The first set is an ingredient set, wild cards. These are extra ingredients with unique circumstances. The second is emotions. This table helps you get more expressive in your cooking. Can you make a sad dish? A happy dish? A pensive dish? This last table is just made of some challenging situations to add to the party.

| First Roll | Second Roll |
|---|---|
| 1 or 2: Wildcard ingredients | 1: Something currently in your fridge |
| | 2: Something currently in your pantry |
| | 3: Buy an ingredient you've never heard of/tasted |
| | 4: Something you hated as a child |
| | 5: Something you love but haven't eaten in years |
| | 6: Anything you can think of |
| 3 or 4: Emotions | 1: Happy |
| | 2: Pensive |
| | 3: Angry |
| | 4: Sad |
| | 5: Silly |
| | 6: Comfortable/tranquil |
| 5 or 6: Twists | 1: Roll on one of the ingredient tables, and you can't use that ingredient. |
| | 2: Purchase only the randomized ingredients, nothing else. All other ingredients must be from your current pantry. |
| | 3: The entire dish must be made in two hours. |
| | 4: Use only one Dutch oven to cook the entire meal. |
| | 5: Make it low-fat, low-salt, or low–something else. |
| | 6: Use only ingredients you've borrowed from neighbors and then invite them to share the final meal. |

## How to Play the Game

There really are no rules. Cook whatever you want. However . . .

- The idea is to roll on the three main ingredient tables to get a meat; a fruit, veggie, or starch; and a flavoring.
- Use those ingredients in any way, and in any form, and in any combination.
- Use any additional ingredients that you want in any way, form, or combination.
- Use any cooking method you like. This *is* a Dutch oven cookbook, so I'd encourage you go use your Dutch ovens, but, hey, it's your backyard or kitchen. Really, there are no rules.
- Use the wildcard table any way you want to. Make it an optional additional roll. You could decide to try the emotions table with the other ingredients. Or just to add in one of the twists. There are no rules. Did I mention that already?
- Share what you cook! Let others taste it. Take pictures and put it up on Facebook. Tweet it on Twitter! Post the recipe you end up with on your blog! Or on my blog at marksblackpot.com!

## Some Examples

So, here are some examples of how the tables might work:

- My first roll on the meat table is a 6, then a 4. That's "Dried Meats."
- Then, on the veggie table is a 3, then a 4. That's "Yellow Squash or zucchini."
- Finally, on the flavoring table, a 3 and then a 2: "Cilantro."

So, what I might do is to slice up some fresh zucchini and bread the "coins" with egg and crackers, then fry them to "al dente" in a Dutch oven. Then make a sort of pesto-ish sauce with oil, cilantro, and other spices and herbs, and mix in some finely chopped turkey jerky.

## Another Try

- On the meat table, I roll a 4, 2. A quick check reveals: "Chicken."
- For the veggies, I roll 5, then a 3. That's "Tomatoes."
- A 5, then a 1 on the flavorings table is "Lemon Juice."

- Finally, on the wild table, I roll a double 4. This is supposed to be a "sad" dish.

This will be a tough one. Chicken, tomatoes and lemons are all kind of lighter fare, with bright flavors. How can you make that taste sad? Maybe if you made the tomatoes and the lemons into a sauce with a harsh and bitter edge, using herbs, salt and pepper. Then, perhaps, bread and fry the chicken so that it's heavier. An interesting challenge.

### CHALLENGE RECIPES

Now, here are some recipes of some dishes that I've made doing random ingredients and other challenges like these.

## APPLE-ORANGE HAM

"You can't compare apples to oranges!" So the saying goes.

Well, in this Dutch oven challenge, we won't compare. Instead, we will combine.

I got to thinking about these two fruits and how much I love the luscious flavors of each one. I started thinking how much I love to combine savory meats and sweet flavors together onto the same dish. So, here's the challenge I issued.

Prepare a dish using the following ingredients:

- apples (in any form)
- oranges (in any form)
- any meat (some kind of meat must be included)
- mint (in any form)

The result was Apple-Orange Ham.

I had actually tried to make a dish for the challenge about three weeks before or so, but it didn't turn out well. It wasn't *bad*, but it wasn't what I wanted, and it certainly wasn't as cool as some of the other entries. I did a pan-fried ham steak with an attempt at an orange-apple glaze. In the end it was good, but not great. I will try it again!

But then, for our big family Thanksgiving dinner, I was asked to do a ham. An idea started forming, so I gave it a shot. It turned out to be really, really yummy. It did have several steps to the process, but overall it was fairly easy. The spices played pretty nicely together. I did stick with pretty much the sweet end of the spice spectrum, though. I didn't get too crossover-crazy with the savories.

### TOOLS

14-inch deep Dutch oven
14–16 coals below
16–18 coals above

### INGREDIENTS

oil
2 apples
cloves, whole
1 spiral-sliced, precooked ham, thawed

1 (15-oz.) can Mandarin oranges with syrup
½ can orange juice concentrate
1 apple, minced
zest of 1 orange
½ tsp. cinnamon
½ tsp. nutmeg
½ tsp. fennel
1½ cups brown sugar
minced fresh mint

**I STARTED** out by lighting up some coals. I got one of my big 14-inch deep Dutch ovens out and oiled it inside and out. I put that on a lot of coals, with some on the lid as well, to preheat and to set some of the seasoning on the patina.

While the Dutch oven was heating up, I cut up the apples. I sliced them very thin. I didn't have any whole cloves, so I just sprinkled some ground cloves onto the apple slices and stirred them up really well.

The ham had been thawing in the fridge for almost a week. I cut open the bag and drained it, then put the ham on a plate on the counter, lying on its side. I inserted the apple slices into the spiral slices of the ham. If I had been using whole cloves, I would have inserted them as well. I kinda staggered them from layer to layer. That kept it from bulging out too much. I did that on both sides and then put it in the Dutch oven to cook.

I cooked it for about 2 hours. After about an hour, I made the glaze by mixing the second set of ingredients. It wasn't as thick as I wanted it to be, but it still worked.

I did try something new. The nutmeg was whole, and freshly grated, and the fennel was ground in my mortar and pestle. The smell of the nutmeg as I was grating it was *in-cred-i-ble*.

So, I basted about ¾ of the glaze onto the top of the ham in the last 45 minutes or so of the roasting and let it settle in. About 15 minutes before taking it off the coals, I put the last of the glaze on.

When it was all done, it tasted delicious. I could taste all of the flavors intermingling. I also made a loaf of spice bread and added some dried cranberries. That was really delicious too, and both dishes were a hit with the family.

## SWEET AND SAVORY PORK CHOPS

### TOOLS

12-inch Dutch oven
12 coals below
12 coals above

8-inch or 10-inch Dutch oven
10–12 coals below

**INGREDIENTS**

**The Meat**
6–8 pork chops (I used boneless)

salt
pepper
paprika
chili powder (not too much)
garlic powder (a little extra)

4 medium-to-large potatoes

1–2 lbs. bacon

**The Sauce**
2 peaches
2 handfuls of grapes (I used white grapes)
1 cup water
¼ cup sugar
nutmeg
cinnamon
juice of ½ lemon
lemon zest

**THE FIRST** thing I did was to thaw the meat. I actually had it in the fridge for several days, so that wasn't a problem. I took the pork chops out and patted them dry. Then I mixed up the spices in the second set of ingredients. You can use any spice rub that you like. I started with equal amounts of salt, pepper, and paprika and then added the chili powder and the garlic powder.

I mixed up the spices in a zip-top baggie, shook it up, and added the meat. I shook those up and then pulled them out and shook off the excess. I let these sit for a while in the fridge.

While my coals were heating up, I chopped up the potatoes. I quartered them and then sliced them kinda thin. These went into the bottom of the Dutch oven.

I pulled out the seasoned pork chops and wrapped each one tightly in two strips of bacon. Then, I laid that on top of the potatoes. With all of the pork chops wrapped and in place, I took the Dutch oven out and got it on the coals.

Then I turned my attention to the sauce. I sliced up the peaches, thin, and chopped up the grapes and put those in the smaller Dutch oven. I added some water and then the sugar, nutmeg, cinnamon, lemon juice, and lemon zest. That went out on the coals too. At first, I covered it with the lid so it would heat up to a boil faster. Then I removed the lid so it would start to simmer and reduce.

About halfway through, I realized that I had mismanaged my coals and that it was going to burn out. I hurriedly lit up some more, but the coals were almost completely burned out before the new ones were ready. Still, I managed to get some fresh coals on and keep it cooking in time. It's frustrating when I catch myself not paying attention!

The end result was absolutely delicious. The potatoes were both soft and crisp, and they were seasoned slightly from the drippings of the bacon and pork chops. The chops themselves were amazing. I served them, still wrapped, with the fruit sauce on top.

## DIETARY CHALLENGE SALMON

I had an interesting Dutch oven cooking challenge one week. My family and I have been traveling cross-country to visit my parents in Indiana. My folks are getting a bit "on in years," and we came out to visit and help out.

Mom especially has been quite thrilled by my books, so Jodi encouraged me to bring a Dutch oven out with us so I could cook for them one night. We all decided it would be great to do it in celebration of my dad's birthday. The tricky part is, both Mom and Dad have some quite specialized dietary needs. Mom gets sores in her mouth, so she can't eat things that are too acidic, or even too salty. Neither of them can have foods that are too fatty, and Dad can't have too much sodium (the salt thing again).

For his birthday, Dad chose salmon.

So, here are my parameters:

1: a salmon dish, with small portions

2: little or no salt

3: for Mom, little or no acidic flavors

4: little oil or fats

5: still have it be flavorful and visually appealing

6: do it all in only one Dutch oven

That all added up to quite a challenge. I tackled the challenge and came through nicely. I baked a loaf of swirled bread. Then I roasted some potato chunks and finally cooked the salmon pieces atop the potatoes. The fish was served topped with a salad of fresh sweet peppers and other veggies.

As I cooked it, however, and as I thought about it afterward, I came up with a way to make it even more flavorful and robust, and while staying better in the parameters. Here's that plan:

**TOOLS**
12-inch shallow Dutch oven
15–18 coals below, for the sautéing
22–24 coals below, for the next step
10–12 coals below and 16–18 above, for the final salmon bake

**INGREDIENTS**
1 medium yellow onion
2 sweet peppers, different colors
2 stalks celery
2 Roma tomatoes
3–4 cloves fresh garlic
dash of salt
1 Tbsp. butter

4–5 portions salmon
1 Tbsp. butter
liberal shakes of thyme, sage, cilantro
dash of salt
dash of pepper

6–8 small red potatoes
dash of salt
dash of pepper
dash of paprika
1 Tbsp. butter

**THE FIRST** step is to light up the coals and get the Dutch oven ready to sauté the veggies. Get the Dutch oven really hot. While that is heating up and readying, dice up the veggies and mince the garlic. My idea is to sweeten the onions and tame and enrich the flavors of the veggies by sautéing them in butter. Start with the onions and the garlic. Once they're translucent, add the peppers. Finally, add the celery and tomatoes. Once the veggies are done (and I'd go until there is some caramelization on the onions), pull them out of the Dutch oven and set them aside.

While the veggies are cooking, season the salmon with the flavorings, and quarter the potatoes (I leave the skin on).

Then, refresh the coals and get the Dutch oven really hot again, still using just bottom heat. Really turn up the heat. Melt the butter on the bottom of the Dutch oven, then put the salmon fillets on. It should sizzle and sear instantly. After a minute or two, turn them over and let the other side sear. Let each side get a good brown going on. Since you won't have a lot of salt to carry the flavor, you'll use the sear and the herbs instead.

When the salmon is nicely brown, but not necessarily cooked all the way through, pull it off. Melt the last of the butter and toss in the potatoes, with their seasonings. Stir it all up, to evenly coat everything. Adjust the coals for a 350-degree bake, and set the oven on the heat.

After about 10 minutes, the potatoes will be starting to cook through but not done yet. Layer the salmon pieces on top of them and the sautéed veggies on top of the salmon. Bake it for another 10–15 minutes.

And there you'll have it! A delicious, flavorful meal, with relatively little fat, sodium, and acidic flavors, all cooked in a single Dutch oven.

## DECONSTRUCTION

Another challenge that I started to explore was deconstruction. It really helped me to think through a dish and get to its core so I could pick it apart and rebuild it. I learned a lot about each dish and about myself!

### Deconstructing Deconstruction

"What do all those cooking shows mean when they say that the dish was 'deconstructed'? I just don't get it!"

If you've ever asked yourself or anyone else this question, read on!

In the last few years, the food world has been abuzz with the word "deconstruction," and it has been applied and interpreted in many, many different ways. Maybe you heard one of the commentators on *Iron Chef* talk about someone doing a "deconstruction," or maybe you saw it on a menu in a trendy restaurant. What does it mean? In fact, that depends a lot on who you talked to last.

It's really a way for a chef to challenge himself or herself and create something new out of something common. It's also a great way to explore the art of food. More on that in a minute.

Here's a general understanding of what it means when a chef "deconstructs" a dish:

- The chef chooses a common, popular, or well-known dish. He or she could choose a rare or new dish, but then, what would be the point?
- The chef looks over the ingredients of that dish and contemplates how they combine in the original dish.
- The chef uses those ingredients and prepares them and combines them in different ways to create a wholly new dish and a completely new edible experience. Sometimes that results in a new dish that evokes the experience of the original, and sometimes that results in a whole new experience for the taster.

Now, there are all kinds of ways to approach this. One is to stick with the initial ingredients and not change them up or add anything. Another is to use them as the core and develop outward from there. Sometimes, you use some traditional preparations, and, other times, you step out on a limb. The idea, as a chef, as a creator of a culinary experience, is that you try something new, based on something old.

The confusion in the term comes when some restaurants simply plate the dish in a different way, or separate out the ingredients and serve them to you that way, and then call it "deconstructed" so that you can see that they're hip and trendy. Or when a home cook hears about deconstruction on a food network show and simply mixes all of the ingredients together. Really, the idea is to dig deep and try to think of something entirely new. It's a time of discovery and a time to push yourself. It's a time to make mistakes, sure, and a time to find new understanding.

Here's an example of one quick way a deconstruction could happen. Take a traditional apple pie. Here are the core ingredients:

**The Crust:**
flour
shortening
water

**The Filling:**
apples
spices
sugar

**Plating:**
ice cream
chocolate sauce

What are some of the ways you could recombine these elements?

How about putting the sugar and spices on fresh apples (rather than cooked), and resting them on a bed of ice cream, with crumbled crust over the top? How about blending the ice cream, the apples, and the spices into a shake or a smoothie, and dabbing that on crust squares, like crackers, maybe with the chocolate drizzled over the top?

These are just a few quick suggestions. What could you add to it? What could you take away? How could it be done uniquely and new? This is the real art and challenge of deconstruction.

So I chose some food deconstruction challenges. For me, it's a chance to stretch myself as a chef and to really explore art and the nature of self-discovery and self-expression. These were the rules of the deconstruction challenges:

- Start by planning well. Contemplate the ingredients of the original dish. Contemplate new ways of treating them, preparing them, combining them.
- Create a new dish using those ingredients. You may choose to add ingredients. You may choose to only use the original set. It's up to you. Explore. See how far you can get from the original dish, or see how you can remain true to its basic character. Learn.
- Blog about it. Explain your approach and your thoughts. Remember to interlink.

The first challenge was the classic child's PB&J.

**INGREDIENTS**
bread (flour, salt, yeast, water, honey)
peanut butter (peanuts, salt, sugar, various nasty and complex chemicals)
grape jelly (grapes, pectin, sugar, more mutagenic chemicals)

Shake it up! See what comes out! Share!

My friend John, at mormonfoodie.com, came up with a peanut butter–filled ravioli with a jelly sauce, topped with sprinkled powdered sugar. I was amazed. That, however, will have to wait for another book. Here was what I came up with.

## MARK AND JODI'S P.B. AND J. DECONSTRUCTION DESSERT

When I first approached this challenge, I was a bit at a loss. I did have some ideas, but they weren't really coming together. I talked with my wife about a few of them, and none of them seemed to impress her, either.

Part of my dilemma was to decide what part of the meal it would be. My ideas didn't seem to be substantial enough to make it a main dish, and it was too weird to be a side dish. I mean, what sort of main dish would a PB&J go with? It's not like picking a good wine for your meal. There are no rules here.

I finally settled on the idea of it being a dessert. That felt right. It would work. But then, how to do it? Nothing I thought of really worked in my head, and nothing seemed to appeal to my wife, either. Then she mentioned something about peanut butter cookies. I ran through those ingredients in my head (like peanut butter, of course, and flour and egg for the bread), and it started to snap into place. A dessert, based on the cookie, with a glaze of the jelly on top!

Then I started thinking about chocolate. I don't usually add chocolate to my PB&Js. But, I thought, it's my dish—I can add to it as I please. I decided to do some sort of chocolate crumb crust below the cookie. Jodi suggested a chocolate sauce on top, which I initially resisted. But who can resist a chocolate sauce for long? I mean, get real! It really turned out to be the perfect topper.

In the end, it really did taste great, and it evoked the flavors of the original, while taking it to a new place. That's the goal of deconstruction, isn't it? A success!

Plus, I learned to pay more attention to my wife! Here it all is:

### TOOLS

10-inch Dutch oven
8–10 coals below, 12–14 coals above

8-inch Dutch oven
8–10 coals below

### INGREDIENTS

**The Crust**
1 package graham crackers

¼ cup brown sugar
1 small brick of baker's chocolate
2 Tbsp. cocoa powder
6 Tbsp. melted butter

**The Cookie Center**
½ cup shortening
¾ cup peanut butter (crunchy or smooth)
⅓ cup granulated sugar
⅓ cup brown sugar
1 egg
2 Tbsp. milk
1 tsp. vanilla extract
1½ cups flour
1 tsp. baking soda
½ tsp. salt

**The Jelly Topping**
1 cup grape jelly
1 tsp. cinnamon
1 tsp. nutmeg
1 tsp. mint leaves
½ tsp. ground fennel seeds

**To Drizzle**
8 oz. chocolate chips
½ cup heavy whipping cream

**I STARTED** out by lighting up the coals. Once they were getting a little white, I put some on the 10-inch Dutch oven lid to begin preheating it. Actually, I did that part somewhere in between working on the ingredients.

The next step was to chop up the graham crackers. I actually used a blender. Jodi mocked me because I usually try not to use electrical appliances when I Dutch oven. She thinks that's silly, but since they are not allowed in cook-offs, I try not to use them at home as much as possible. But this time I was going to be using a table mixer for the cookie anyway, so I figured I could use a blender for the crackers too. I mixed in the other crust ingredients and pressed the resulting chocolate mud into the bottom of the 10-inch Dutch oven.

Then I mixed all of the other cookie center ingredients in the table mixer, whipping it up nicely. I spread that over the crumbs, being careful not to disturb that level as I did.

Finally, I mixed the topping ingredients and spread that in a thin layer over the top. By this time, the lid was pretty hot, so I went out and adjusted the coals, top and bottom, and began baking it.

I didn't know what to expect, so I checked it about every 10–15 minutes. It ended up baking for 30–45 minutes. The center was the last part to cook, and it was pretty jiggly right up to the end. When that was pretty solid, I took it off the coals and brought it inside. Then I went on cooking the rest of the meal, which was a basic chicken and potatoes pot with biscuits on the side.

When it became close to time to serve dessert, I still hadn't decided on the chocolate sauce. Jodi made the choice for me and cooked it up. If I had done it in the Dutch ovens, I would have used pretty much the same process she did, but simply done it in my 8-inch Dutch oven. I would have added the two ingredients and stirred them until the chips melted and it all blended with the cream. Easy, quick, and delicious.

As I said, it turned out to be the perfect topping! Really, the dessert was great. It was a perfect combination of the flavors of the traditional peanut butter and jelly sandwich, while adding the chocolate and the other flavors to take it in a new direction.

## DECONSTRUCTED JAMBALAYA HAM

My father-in-law bought us a ham for Christmas dinner one year, and I was contemplating how to make it. I've got a lot of ham recipes already, and I was tempted to just do one of those again. But I also thought about doing it differently.

To get some ideas, I browsed the web. As I was doing a search, I saw a recipe for a jambalaya with ham chunks in it. I looked it over and thought I could deconstruct it.

In this case, the thought was to roast the ham with all the herbs and seasonings, flavoring it, and then to combine all of the veggie ingredients around the ham and to use the veggies and liquids as a baste to flavor the ham roast.

I was a bit nervous to do it. My father-in-law is a very traditional eater, and I wasn't sure how he'd go for it, and my wife was even less convinced when I explained what I'd be doing. I decided to go ahead with it anyway.

**TOOLS**
14-inch Dutch oven
18 coals below
18 coals above

**INGREDIENTS**
1 (8-lb.) ham, thawed

**Liberal shakes of**
salt
pepper
parsley
thyme
basil
bay leaves
paprika
cayenne pepper (not much, to taste)

3 medium onions, diced
3 sweet peppers
4 medium tomatoes, diced
3 stalks celery, chopped
5 cloves garlic, coarsely chopped

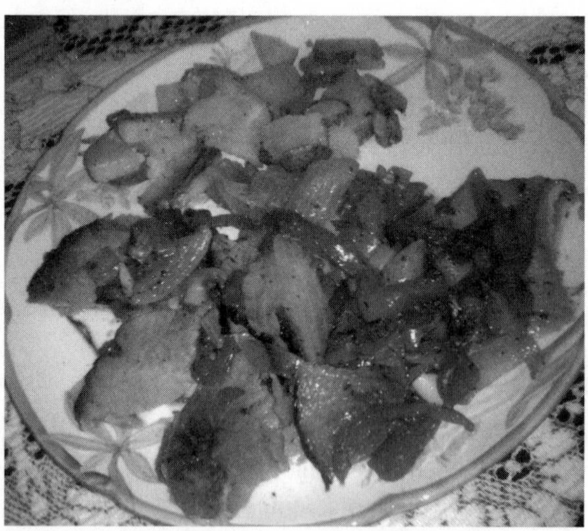

**I STARTED** out with the thawed ham (which was spiral cut, precooked). I cut it out of the package and put it into the 14-inch Dutch oven without letting it drain, to keep as much of the liquid as possible. I mixed all of the seasonings in a bowl and mixed them up, then rubbed them all over the ham. I put that onto the coals.

I waited only about a half hour to begin chopping up and prepping the veggies. When they were all ready, I tossed them in around the ham.

I made sure that I had plenty of fresh coals ready to keep coming in from time to time from the side fire.

When the veggies had been in for a half hour or so, I began scooping the cooking veggies and liquids up and spooning it over the ham every 20 minutes or so. I also started thinking about a side dish. I had bread from another day and some salad, but I wanted a bit more variety. I decided to do some roasted seasoned potatoes.

### SIMPLE ROASTED POTATOES

#### TOOLS

10-inch Dutch oven
10 coals below
10–12 coals above

#### INGREDIENTS

4 large potatoes
olive oil
salt
pepper
paprika

**I STARTED** by chopping up the potatoes thin. I poured the olive oil on them in the 10-inch Dutch oven and added the seasonings. I stirred it up well and put it on the coals.

From then on, it was easy. I just monitored the coals and the temperature of the ham, and got it on the table when it was done. The roast cooked for a total of about 2½ hours.

The verdict? I loved it, my wife loved it, and even my father-in-law asked to take some home!

## DECONSTRUCTED HAMBURGER SALAD

The next challenge I chose was a deconstruction of the basic, traditional American hamburger.

One thing I learned was that I need to start paying more attention to myself when I make these challenges. I really struggled with this one as well. I struggled with how to use all of those basic ingredients and make it fresh and new.

The basic ingredients:

- ground beef
- ketchup
- mustard
- cheddar cheese
- onions
- pickles
- lettuce
- mayonnaise
- and, of course, the bun

I bounced a number of ideas around in my head and wrestled with all of them. On the way, I realized that there is one type of dish that is significantly underrepresented in my other books and on my blog: the salad.

There's a reason for that: You usually don't cook salads, and Dutch ovens are a pot for cooking things. I suppose you could throw some lettuce and sliced/chopped veggies into a cold Dutch oven, toss it with some dressing, and serve it as is!

Still, you can cook some elements of a salad. That's one reason I love big chef's salads. With meat, veggies, and seasonings, they can be a whole meal themselves. So, I decided to try this one that way. The hamburger salad!

The lettuce goes from a simple topping on the hamburger to the basis of the dish. The meat, on the other hand, becomes the topping! What about the bun? I turned that into croutons! The sauces of the hamburger (ketchup, mustard, mayo) combined with other spices to make a dressing for both the meat and the rest of the salad.

## THE CROUTONS

### TOOLS

12-inch Dutch oven
10–12 coals below
14–16 coals above

### INGREDIENTS

1 stick butter

4–6 hamburger buns
seasoning salt
pepper

## THE MEAT AND SAUCE

### TOOLS

12-inch Dutch oven
22 coals below

### INGREDIENTS

1 onion
4 cloves garlic
olive oil
2 lbs. ground beef
salt
pepper

½ cup ketchup
about 3 Tbsp. mustard
about 2 Tbsp. mayonnaise
1 Tbsp. dill relish
cayenne pepper
salt
pepper

## THE SALAD

### INGREDIENTS

1 head iceberg lettuce (or other greens)
1–2 tomatoes
grated cheddar cheese

**OF ALL** the elements for this dish, I was the least confident in the croutons, so I started with those. I lit up some coals, and, when they got white, I put them under one of the 12-inch Dutch ovens. I put in the butter to melt while I sliced up the buns. I did them in long, narrow strips, almost looking like french fries. I think that next time I'll just cube them so they look a little more like traditional croutons. They'll be easier to stir and handle.

Once the butter had melted, I shook in a liberal amount of the seasoning salt, maybe a teaspoon's worth. I added the pepper the same way, maybe a little less. I tossed in the sliced bread and stirred it thoroughly to coat each piece in butter and seasoning.

I actually had fewer coals on as I started, but I could soon see that it needed to be hotter to get the toasty brown I wanted. So I upped the numbers, as listed. I kept the lid on and stirred the bread strips frequently to keep them browning but not burning.

I got some more coals under another 12-inch Dutch oven, and I diced the onion and minced the garlic. I poured in some olive oil to heat up, then tossed in the garlic and onions with a little salt. They started sizzling immediately, and I let them sauté.

When they were getting a bit brown, I put in the ground beef to brown as well. Add the salt and pepper to taste.

While that was cooking, I mixed up the sauce. I started with the ketchup, and that was really the only one that I measured. The rest I just mixed in and tasted as I went. I was simply striving for a balance of flavors.

I stirred it up and then poured it in with the meat. I stirred that and let it cook for a little, but not much. I wanted it to be a part of the meat, but not to evaporate or reduce.

Finally, the meat was done, the croutons were nicely roasted and brown, and it was time to assemble the salad

I started by shredding the lettuce and dicing the tomatoes. I used the lettuce as the base of the dish and then added tomatoes on top. I spooned meat liberally over the base and sprinkled some croutons on top of that. Finally, I topped it by grating some cheddar on top.

My whole family pronounced this one a success! I was pleased too, not only because I enjoyed the taste, but also because it was a new take on the burger (for me, anyway), yet it still maintained a lot of the original burger taste. It had some salty and sour tones, and some sweet from the ketchup in the sauce. The lettuce, of course, had a hint of a bitter tone, and its texture made it feel like a salad.

**AT THE** beginning of this book, I wrote about cooking as an art form and as a means of expression. It's times like these that I have to dig down inside myself and find ideas and translate them into ingredients and flavors to evoke an experience. When I'm just cooking someone else's recipe, I might learn a lot, or I might make a delicious dish, but I'm not fully expressing *me*. Try these challenges, and you may discover some interesting parts of yourself that you didn't know before!

# BONUS CHAPTER: A BIG FEAST

## Planning and Preparing a Full Seven-Course Dutch Oven Feast

In early 2008, I got this interesting idea bugging around in my mind that I should really put my Dutch oven skills to the test. I was going to plan and cook a full seven-course meal and serve it up to my friends as a triumph of my abilities thus far. I would plan and practice the dishes, and on the great and dreadful day, I would start at 8 o'clock in the morning and cook until the guests arrived that evening.

I had a blast digging for recipes and trying to find the ones that would be perfect for the day. Some of them I tried out first, and others I just planned in.

The day came, and I cooked away. It was tiring, but also energizing. I have a tough time thinking of a day where I had more fun cooking. It was a test for me, but not like the pressure of a cook-off. It had a whole different feel.

The evening went perfectly.

The following year, I did it again. It was much easier that year. I had gotten much better at cooking and at managing multiple pots and multiple dishes concurrently. I planned the day and the dishes out with a time chart, broken down into half-hour increments, separated by dish/course so at any time I could tell what I needed to be doing.

This was the menu for The Feast 2009:

- Appetizer: cheese, crackers, and veggies with dip. Simple stuff. Simple is good, because fancy is comin' up . . .
- Soup: Steve's chicken soup. I did it basically as he did, but I had this idea to dress it up with chicken and shrimp grilled on skewers and set across the bowl! It's hard to describe, but I could see it in my head.
- Salad: spinach, mozzarella, and tomato salad. Another one that looked really cool!
- Bread: braided bread with orange glaze. The same bread I tried the previous year but fumbled.
- Main dish: crown roast. I swear, in all the world of meats, there isn't anything that can compare with a crown roast for sheer "wow" factor. At first, I didn't know if I'd do a stuffing or not. I also ended up doing a citrus-draped turkey so there would be more meat for all the guests.
- Vegetable: I was originally going to do a dish of roasted potatoes and asparagus. In the end I put the veggies around the roast in the Dutch oven and just served them on the side.
- Drink: Sprite with orange juice.
- Dessert: banana bread with chocolate and cinnamon butter sauces. And whipped cream, as if that weren't enough.

There was a citrus theme running through the whole meal, in the soup, the glaze on the bread, the roast and the turkey, and the drink. I even put mandarin orange slices on the salad. It nicely tied the whole meal together.

Now, this was back in 2009, so I'm relying on old blog posts and memory for these recipes. I don't have my old copies of the time plan, either. But here's how it all came off . . .

I made the hors d'oeuvres the night before. I simply sliced up cheeses, cold cuts, and arranged them nicely with crackers. It was fun to serve up as the guests arrived and began visiting.

The soup was the first course that was served at the table. Here's the recipe and the process, from when my friend Steven did it at the IDOS Taste of Dutch cooking demo.

## CHICKEN SOUP WITH RICE

### TOOLS
12-inch Dutch Oven
15–20 coals below

### INGREDIENTS
3 potatoes, cubed
2 carrots, sliced
2 celery stalks, sliced
2 cups cubed chicken, cooked
1 (14-oz.) can tomatoes with liquid
¼ cup rice
1 Tbsp. salt
½ tsp. thyme
¼ tsp. basil
1 bay leaf
⅛ tsp. pepper
8 cups water

**I PUT** all of the ingredients in the pot, and then I put it on the coals and brought it to boil. This took a while, and it was easier covered. Then, I pulled off some coals, just enough to keep it simmering for 45 minutes. With all those veggies, and 8 cups of water, you could serve a lot of people with this Dutch oven chicken soup.

The day of the feast, I tweaked it up a bit:

- I added a sliced-up jalapeño. With this much stuff in the soup, one pepper will give it some zing without burning. To keep it tame, seed and core the jalapeño before you slice it.
- Lemon juice gave it a delicious Mediterranean flavor and tied it in with the citrus theme. I gave it as much as ¼–½ cup, given the amount of water in this recipe.
- I put some shrimp on skewers and grilled them. When I served the soup, I set the plate in front of the guest, then laid the skewer of shrimp across the bowl, above the soup. It was a classy presentation!

Thanks, Steve, for your soup idea!

**THE NEXT** course was the salad course. I used large spinach leaves, tomatoes sliced in circles, rings of fresh raw onion, and circles of sliced mozzarella arranged on the plates to emphasize the circles. Then I tossed on some mandarin orange slices and some raisins, and drizzled with an oriental ginger dressing. It was impressive to look at and delicious.

## ORANGE-GLAZED SOURDOUGH BREAD

I brought the bread to the table alongside the main dishes. Here's the bread recipe. It is a sourdough recipe, so I had to catch some yeast germs and make a sourdough starter first. I did this by leaving equal amounts of flour and water out in the open air for several days. Each day I would swap half of the goo out for equal amounts of fresh flour and water goo. Finally, one day, it was foamy and bubbly, signifying that I had caught some wild yeast. I fed it again and stored it, covered, in the fridge.

### TOOLS

12-inch Dutch oven
18 coals above
9–10 coals below

### INGREDIENTS

**The Sponge**
1 cup sourdough starter
2½ cups hot water
4 cups flour

**The Dough**
1 cup flour (with as much as 2–3 more cups during kneading)
1 egg
2 Tbsp. sugar
3 Tbsp. oil
1 Tbsp. salt

oil

**The Glaze**
1 orange
cinnamon
1 frozen canister orange juice concentrate (any size—you won't use it all)

**THE NIGHT** before, I made the sponge. I took a few globs of goo from the starter I had in the fridge and mixed it with equal amounts of flour and water. I needed enough new goo to make a cup full of starter. I set it aside for a few hours to wake up and get good and frothy with yeast bugs.

Then, I mixed all the ingredients in the sponge set and stirred it up with a wooden spoon. Metal utensils react with the yeast. I put that aside and covered it with plastic and went to bed.

The next day, I mixed in the dough ingredients. Then I turned it out onto a floured tabletop and started kneading, adding flour as I went. As long as the bread was too sticky, I kept adding flour and kneading it into the ball.

Every once in a while, I did the windowpane test. I grabbed a piece of the dough, flattened it, and stretched it out into a translucent "windowpane." The first few times, it shredded and tore quickly. That meant that the gluten hadn't developed enough yet, and it needed more kneading. Finally, it pulled without tearing, and I knew that it was ready.

Then I sprayed oil in the bowl and put in the dough ball. I sprayed that over with oil and set it aside to rise.

Then I worked on other dishes.

After a couple of hours, I could see that it had risen. Then, I punched it down and stretched it out into three long ropes. I braided these and curled them into the oiled bottom of the Dutch oven. I set it aside to proof (rise again).

Then I lit up a buncha coals.

Once those were white, I brought out the lid and put 18–20 of them on the lid. About 10 minutes later, I could tell the lid was really hot, and the dough in the pot part of the Dutch oven had risen just a little more. I put the Dutch oven out on some coals and put the lid on top. Then it was just a matter of keeping it hot and rotating the Dutch oven every 15 minutes or so.

While it was in the first cooking stage, I mixed up the glaze. I zested the orange and then juiced half of it into the zest. I added the cinnamon to taste. Then I mixed in some orange juice concentrate and kept mixing until it was a smooth but thick glaze. By then the bread was about 20 minutes in, or about half done. I went out and brushed the glaze over the top of the bread and also stuck in the thermometer. Then I closed it all back up and let it cook for about 20 minutes more. At that point the thermometer said about 190 degrees, which is perfect for a light white bread.

I brought it in and let it cool. The glaze smelled and looked wonderful, even if it did make it a little tricky to slide out of the Dutch oven.

## CITRUS CROWN ROAST OF PORK

Sadly, the recipe for the crown roast, the centerpiece of the whole experience, is lost forever. I looked back through my blog over and over, and I can't find it. I did it in the 14-inch deep Dutch oven, surrounded by veggies. I also filled the crown with oranges and lemons and basted the meat with a variation of the same orange glaze that I used on the bread, along with salt and pepper.

I will never forget that day. I hefted the huge Dutch ovens (the citrus turkey was in the other one), and I lifted the lid off the crown roast oven. The steam wafted up, and everyone leaned up and in to see that delicious crown of pork bones, smothered in oranges. The smell swirled around us all, and we sighed and gasped.

Here is my best recollection of it, strained though my old-man memory may be:

### TOOLS

14-inch deep Dutch oven
14–15 coals below
15–18 coals above

### INGREDIENTS

1 (10- to 14-lb.) crown roast of pork, cut and tied in a circle
salt
black pepper
paprika

1 orange
6 oz. frozen orange juice concentrate
cinnamon
nutmeg
ground cloves

2 lemons
1 orange
1 grapefruit

4–5 potatoes, quartered and sliced, or cubed to ¾-inch cubes
3–4 stalks celery, chopped
2 medium onions, chopped
4 cloves garlic, minced
any other veggies you like: carrots, sweet peppers, and so on

**I DO** remember that I bought the crown roast already cut and tied into a circle. I had to special order it. Normally, I like to learn how to do things myself, but this time, with everything going on, I figured I'd let the pros do the cutting.

I mixed the salt, pepper, and paprika and rubbed it all over the meat. I set it into the Dutch oven and let it set for a while. In the meantime, I mixed the glaze and cut up the citrus. The glaze is simply a matter of zesting the orange, then juicing it, and finally mixing in the concentrate until it's a very thick but fluid glaze. Finally, add in the spices.

The citrus is cut up into chunks. I cut the lemons and orange across the "equator" and then quartered each half. I cut the grapefruit into more pieces to make them about the same size.

I coated the meat with one spreading of the glaze, inside as well as out, and then loaded up the center of the crown with the citrus. Finally, I set it all on the coals to roast.

I don't remember how long I roasted it for. I did keep a thermometer in it, and I shot for 170–180 degrees as a target. Every half hour or so, I would open it up and layer on another spread of the glaze. When it was about half done, or maybe even an hour or so from "done," I put the veggies in around the base of the meat.

Other than that, I just kept fresh coals on it to keep it going. I timed it to be done at service time, when I brought it in and cut it up there at the table. What an impressive display!

**TURKEY WASN'T** a part of the initial plan, but we weren't absolutely sure that we'd have enough meat with the crown roast. Some of our guests weren't sure of their RSVPs, and it wasn't clear how many people would be there. So, we got a Turkey hen, 12–14 lbs., and I did my traditional citrus treatment. It turned out that we did have plenty of meat, but it was also nice for everyone to have an additional choice, and many of the guests had both meats.

I didn't brine the bird for a couple of reasons, one being that I hadn't learned about it yet. But we also decided to cook it the day of the event, so I wouldn't have had time to soak it overnight anyway. However, when I do turkeys, I always brine them now. Always!

Here's how. I gather:

- lots of water

- 1 lb. salt
- 1 lb. brown sugar

The night before, I make up this mix. I start with some hot tap water (maybe a couple of quarts) and dissolve the salt and sugar. I let that cool. I put the thawed turkey into a big, clean cooler/tub, and I pour cold water around it, ending with the salt/sugar water. I also put in some ice. I put that whole thing, with the lid on, in my garage. With the ice and the cooler, as well as all the salt, it's pretty safe from germs. In the winter, the garage gets down into the 30s anyway, so that even helps.

## CITRUS TURKEY

The first time I did this, I got the idea watching the Food Network. When I saw them stuffing oranges and lemons in the bird's body cavity, I got intrigued.

Unfortunately, when I went back a few days later, I couldn't find the recipe. I'd forgotten the show I'd seen it on, as well as the chef's name.

Still, the Net is huge, and after a few searches and a bit of experimenting, I arrived at my usual conglomeration of ingredients, pulled from many different recipes.

The results were staggering. It was moist and tender (most of the time Dutch oven turkeys are), and the delicate hint of lemon and citrus throughout the meat was especially tasty. My guests pronounced it delicious, and my wife said it was the best turkey she'd ever tasted.

### TOOLS

14-inch Dutch oven
12–13 coals below
22–24 coals above

### INGREDIENTS

1 (11- to 13-lb.) hen turkey

**The Baste**

½ cup softened butter
1 lemon
1 Tbsp. garlic, minced
⅛ cup chives or green onions
⅛ cup chopped fresh parsley
big pinch of kosher salt

liberal shakes of coarse ground pepper

**The Stuffing**
1 lemon, cut into pieces
½ medium onion, diced
1 orange, cut into pieces

**The Surrounding Veggies**
1 large potato, quartered and sliced
½ medium onion, sliced
½ cup baby carrots, or sliced carrots
3–4 sprigs celery, sliced
⅛ cup chives/green onions, chopped
⅛ cup chopped fresh parsley

**On Top of It All**
1–2 sliced citrus fruits (lemons, oranges, grapefruit)
more kosher salt
more coarse ground black pepper

**MAKE SURE** that the turkey is well-thawed. About a week in the fridge will do, and a night in the brining bath will pretty much take care of it.

I started by lighting up a lot of coals. You can see from the previous page that we're talking more than 34 total, just to get it started. Once it was cooking too, I developed a system that worked pretty well of transferring on new coals as the old ones burned off. More on that in a minute.

I cut open the plastic turkey bag and let it drain. I put the turkey onto a towel on my kitchen counter. Then, I made the baste. I put the softened butter in a bowl and zested and juiced the lemon. I added the zest and juice to the butter, as well as the remaining baste ingredients. It was pretty easy to mix. I also got the stuffing items prepared.

The stuffing step was pretty easy. I packed the turkey full with stuffing, alternating between the lemons, the onions, and the oranges. I pressed the stuffing in pretty tight, partly to get more there and partly to squeeze it a bit to get more juices flowing from the fruits. Then I put the turkey into my 14-inch Dutch oven. People are sometimes surprised that I can cook a turkey in a Dutch oven, but they're often looking at the 20-plus-pound toms. The smaller bird makes more sense, and it fits better in my oven.

Next, I took my baste and coated the top of the bird with it. I like to poke holes in the skin to allow the baste and the seasonings to seep in. Then I sprinkled it with more kosher salt (I like the bigger granules) and the pepper.

Next, I cut up the surrounding veggies, and packed those in around the bird. Finally, I added the slices of citrus on top and some more kosher salt and black pepper. It was ready for the coals.

About every 20 minutes, I'd pour a few more fresh coals into the metal chimney next to the Dutch oven. Then I'd shake it up to circulate the already lit coals in between the new ones so they'd all get lit. Every so often, as I could see the coals burning down, I'd pull 5–8 larger lit coals from the chimney fire, and add them on top. I'd pull 3–4 and just set them on the bottom. By doing that, the old coals burned out, the new ones came on frequently, and I was able to maintain a 350- to 375-degree temperature throughout. It took 3–4 hours to cook. A little longer than I'd wanted, but it was worth waiting for, and my guests were patient. The last 30 minutes or so, I put a lot of extra coals on the lid, which helped brown the upper skin.

When you take it off the coals, bring it in for everyone to *ooh* and *ah* and sniff over, and let it sit for 10–15 minutes. That'll finish off the cooking and let the meat settle into the juices and the seasonings.

Another hint I learned from the Food Network. When you're carving the turkey, cut off the leg first, then in a deep sweeping cut, take the whole breast off. Set that on the plate and slice it into pieces. That way, not only is it quicker, but everyone gets a bit of the crispy and flavorful skin as well.

## BANANA NUT BREAD SUPREME

Finally, the evening wrapped up with this. It was amazingly delicious. And it's a perfect example of how a pretty basic and normal recipe can easily be kicked up a notch and turned into something amazing without a lot of extra work.

### TOOLS

12-inch Dutch oven
8–10 coals below
15–18 coals above

8-inch Dutch oven
8–10 coals below

### INGREDIENTS

5 large ripe bananas

4 eggs, well beaten
2 cups sugar
1 cup shortening
4 cups flour
2 tsp. baking soda
1 tsp. baking powder
1 tsp. salt
1 cup chopped nuts (walnuts or almonds or whatever)
2 bars of chocolate, chopped

oil
flour

2 sticks butter
1 cup sugar
1–2 Tbsp. cinnamon
chocolate syrup
caramel syrup
whipped cream

**I STARTED** by pureeing the bananas, and then I added the eggs. (There are some who say that when cooking in a Dutch oven, you should eschew powered appliances. In fact, in many cook-offs, they're not allowed. Usually I don't use them myself, preferring to do it by hand. But I decided to use the blender on the bananas. May the gods of iron forgive me. I got over it really fast, though.)

Then I got out a bowl and put in the sugar and the shortening. I got out my pastry cutter and started cutting them together. It didn't take long to mix. Then, I added the rest of the ingredients from the first set and mixed those together. So far, so good. I chose almonds, because my wife and walnuts don't mix. And for the chocolate? Ghirardelli! I chose good chocolate for an extra special taste.

Finally, I poured in the banana and egg mix and stirred it all together. I oiled and floured the bottom and sides of my Dutch oven and poured in the mix.

Somewhere in the process of making everything, I had lit my coals and set a lot of hot coals on the lid to preheat it. When the batter was ready, so was the lid. I put the lid on and baked the bread for 45–60 minutes. I tested its doneness by sticking a knife in it. If it comes out clean, then it's done.

Now, I did all this in the morning. There was a lot of other cooking and prepping going on for the rest of the day, so I didn't want to have to rush that. After I pulled it out of the Dutch oven and cooled it, I wrapped the plate up in plastic so it wouldn't dry out.

Up to this point, it's a good banana bread. But I had to take it to another level. This was to be a fancy dinner, and it needed a fancy ending for that final "wow!"

So, right before serving the dessert, I slipped away from the dinner. In my 8-inch Dutch oven, I melted the butter, dissolved the sugar, and added the cinnamon. I came back in and sliced the banana bread into cake-like wedges. I scooped up some of the cinnamon-butter sauce, put that in the bottom of a shallow bowl, and added the cake on top of that. Then I drizzled the top of the cake with the chocolate and the caramel, making sure to get some drizzled on the bowl too. Finally, some whipped cream on top, and it was onto the table.

That little bit of the cinnamon and the other sauces, combined with the whipped cream, was simple, but it took the banana bread to another level.

**IT'S A** tough job to cook all of that. My guests kept asking, "Are you sure we can't bring something?" I had to keep explaining that the whole point was to see if I could do the whole meal, all in my Dutch ovens. It's a great challenge, and it really made me stretch as a chef.

I learned that I had to plan out the whole day. I actually made a spreadsheet. Each column was a different course or dish, and each row was a half hour in the day. I started with the serving time at the bottom of the page and worked each dish backward through the steps. I knew I could cook some dishes, like the bread and the banana bread, early and set them aside. I actually prepared the salad the night before. I planned each half hour out so I knew I would be working on only one thing at a time and so all of my Dutch ovens would be accounted for. If I hadn't made the plan, I would have been a mess. As it was, I was relaxed and having fun the entire day.

I pulled it off, by the way, with two 14-inch deep ovens, two 12-inch shallow ovens, a 10-inch, and an 8-inch.

# ACKNOWLEDGMENTS

Much, much gratitude . . .

To Mom, who was never afraid to try a new dish and who introduced me to many cuisines from around the world.

To Jodi, who encourages me to cook and supports me as I go off promoting my books.

To Brendon and Jacob, who inspire me and try whatever I cook. Cooking with them is always more fun than cooking alone!

To Andy, for the friendship and the challenges, which help me to learn.

To Ruth and Steven, who have taught me so much and given me so much encouragement.

To John, without whom I never would have started on this adventure. Thanks for the enduring friendship too.

To Omar, Ted, Diane, Colleen, Ranes, Matt, and my many other IDOS friends.

And to my newfound friends at Cedar Fort!

# RESOURCES

- Marksblackpot.com—my blog. It's okay that I mention it first, isn't it?
- Youtube.com/marksblackpot—my own videos and links to lots of other great clips!
- Mormonfoodie.com—John's food blog. Amazing ideas, amazing recipes.
- Backporchgourmet.com—Andy's outdoor cooking blog. Smart and fun to read!
- Logcabingrub.com—Colleen's cookbooks.
- IDOS.org—the home site of the International Dutch Oven Society.
- Dutchovenmadness.blogspot.com—Toni's Dutch oven blog. She started by cooking every night for a year in her Dutch ovens!
- Cedarfort.com—my publishers!

# INDEX

## A



## B

## C



## D



## E

## F



## G



## H



## J



## K



## L



## M

## N



## O



## P



## R



## S

## T



## Y



## Z

# ABOUT THE AUTHOR

**MARK STARTED** cooking in his Dutch ovens in 2006 when his wife surprised him with one as a Father's Day present. His first cooking attempt was pizza, and the family instantly declared it a success! He began a tradition of cooking the family's Sunday dinners in his Dutch ovens.

In April of the following year, he thought he should start sharing what he learned, and he established the Mark's Black Pot blog. Years and hundreds of recipes later, it's still one of the most widely read Dutch oven blogs on the Internet.

Mark lives in Eagle Mountain, Utah, with his wife, Jodi, and two boys, who are also budding chefs.

### OTHER DUTCH OVEN BOOKS BY MARK HANSEN:

***Best of the Black Pot:***
*Must-Have Dutch Oven Favorites*

***Black Pot for Beginners:***
*Surefire Methods to Get a Great Dutch Oven Dish Every Time*